Praise for the
Meditative Commentary
on
Proverbs, Ecclesiastes, and Job

"In the volume *Proverbs, Ecclesiastes, and Job*, Holloway draws the attention of the reader to the wisdom found in the biblical texts. He delineates the rich offerings of the wisdom literature and then leads the readers in an intimate foray into each text through the ancient practice of *lectio divina*. The readings and questions within this work offer a rhythm of daily immersion into the heart and soul of God."

—**Jackie Halstead,** CEO, Selah Center for Spiritual Formation, and author of *Leaning into God's Embrace: A Guidebook for Contemplative Prayer*

"In this book Gary Holloway ably merges his scholarly expertise with his love for congregational Bible study. He deftly introduces Protestant lay audiences to the practice of *lectio divina*, a reading approach to Scripture that quintessentially empowers its readers to hear God speaking meaningfully to them in their everyday lives and calling them to respond obediently in faith. Holloway helps modern believers engage the timeless lessons from the Wisdom literature of the Old Testament."

—**Rick R. Marrs,** Professor of Religion, Pepperdine University

"Bible scholars have shown us the riches that can be gleaned from attending to the history, language, and culture through which Scripture came to us. But Christians have from the beginning listened to Scripture as a word from God that can transform us as we meditate on it—words that transcend their original time and place. Here is a commentary that invites you not to abandon study but to listen with your heart to the heart of God."

—**Randy Harris,** Professor and Spiritual Director, Department of Bible, Missions, and Ministry, Abilene Christian University, and author of *Living Jesus*

PROVERBS, ECCLESIASTES, AND JOB

A MEDITATIVE
COMMENTARY
on the Old Testament

PROVERBS, ECCLESIASTES, AND JOB

GOD GIVES HIS PEOPLE WISDOM

GARY HOLLOWAY

LEAFWOOD
PUBLISHERS
an imprint of Abilene Christian University Press

PROVERBS, ECCLESIASTES, AND JOB
GOD GIVES HIS PEOPLE WISDOM
A Meditative Commentary

LEAFWOOD
PUBLISHERS
an imprint of Abilene Christian University Press

Copyright © 2023 by Gary Holloway

ISBN 978-1-68426-432-2

Printed in the United States of America

ALL RIGHTS RESERVED
No part of this publication may be reproduced, stored in a retrieval system, or transmitted in any form by any means—electronic, mechanical, photocopying, recording, or otherwise—without prior written consent.

Scripture quotations marked NIV are taken from the Holy Bible, New International Version®, NIV®. Copyright ©1973, 1978, 1984, 2011 by Biblica, Inc.™ Used by permission of Zondervan. All rights reserved worldwide.

Scripture quotations marked NLT are taken from the Holy Bible, New Living Translation, copyright ©1996, 2004, 2007, 2015 by Tyndale House Foundation. Used by permission of Tyndale House Publishers, Inc., Carol Stream, IL 60188. All rights reserved.

Scripture quotations marked ESV are from the Holy Bible, English Standard Version®. Copyright © 2001 by Crossway, a publishing ministry of Good News Publishers. ESV® Text Edition: 2016. The ESV® text has been reproduced in cooperation with and by permission of Good News Publishers. All rights reserved.

Cataloging-in-Publication Data is on file at the Library of Congress, Washington, DC.

Cover design by Bruce Gore
Interior text design by Sandy Armstrong, Strong Design

Leafwood Publishers is an imprint of Abilene Christian University Press
For information contact:
ACU Box 29138
Abilene, Texas 79699

1-877-816-4455
www.leafwoodpublishers.com

23 24 25 26 27 28 29 / 7 6 5 4 3 2 1

To Phillip Camp, a man of wisdom

CONTENTS

Introduction 11
   Hearing God in Scripture 11
   The Spirituality of Proverbs, Ecclesiastes, and Job 19

MEDITATIONS
PROVERBS

The Value of Wisdom: 1:1–19 25
Characteristics of Wisdom: Humility 29
Characteristics of Wisdom: Honesty 33
Characteristics of Wisdom: Diligence in Work 37
Characteristics of Wisdom: Wise Speech 43
Characteristics of Wisdom: Wealth, Poverty, and Justice 47
Characteristics of Wisdom: Family 53
Characteristics of Wisdom: Friendship 59
Wisdom Personified: Lady Wisdom—8:1–9:6 63
A Lifetime of Wisdom: 31:10–31 69

MEDITATIONS
ECCLESIASTES

The Limits of Wisdom: 1:1–18 75
The Limits of Work: 2:4–26 79
The Limits of Timing: 3:1–4:6 85
The Limits of Wealth: 5:8–6:9 91
Wisdom Limited by Age: 11:7–12:8 97

MEDITATIONS
JOB

The Lord Notices Job: 1:1–22 103
Job Told to Curse God: 2:1–3:26 109
Job's Friends Blame Job: 4:1–21; 6:1–30 115
Job Maintains His Innocence: 31:1–40 121
The Lord Answers Job: 38:1–11; 40:1–5; 42:1–17 127

INTRODUCTION
HEARING GOD IN SCRIPTURE

There are many commentaries, guides, and workbooks on the various books of the Bible. How is this series different? It is not intended to answer all your scholarly questions about the Bible, or even make you an expert in the details of Scripture. Instead, this series is designed to help you hear the voice of God for your everyday life. It is a guide to meditation on the Bible, meditation that will allow the Bible to transform you.

We read in many ways. We might scan the newspaper for information, read a map for location, read a novel for pleasure, or read a textbook to pass a test. These are all good ways to read, depending on our circumstances.

A young soldier far away from home who receives a letter from his wife reads in yet another way. He might scan the letter quickly at first for news and information. But his longing for his beloved causes him to read the letter again and again, hearing her sweet voice in every line. He slowly treasures each word of this precious letter.

Bible Study

So also, there are many good ways to read the Bible, depending on our circumstances. Bible study is absolutely necessary for our life with God. We rightly study the Bible for information. We ask: Who wrote this? When was it written? Who were the original readers? How do these words apply to me? More importantly, we want information about God. Who is he? What does he think of me? What does he want from me?

There is no substitute for this kind of close, dedicated Bible study. We must know what the Bible says to know our standing with God. We therefore read the Bible to discover true doctrine or teaching. But some, in their emphasis on the authority and inspiration of the Bible, have forgotten that Bible study is not an end in itself. We want to know God through Scripture. We want to have a relationship with the Teacher, not just the teachings.

Jesus tells some of God's people in his day, "You study the Scriptures diligently because you think that in them you possess eternal life. These are the very Scriptures that testify about me, yet you refuse to come to me to have life" (John 5:39–40 NIV). He's not telling them to study their Bibles less; he is reminding them of the deeper purpose of Bible study—to draw us to God through Jesus. Bible study is a means, not an end.

Yet the way many of us have learned to study the Bible may actually get in the way of hearing God. "Bible study" may sound a lot like schoolwork, and many of us were happy to get out of school. "Bible study" may call to mind pictures of intellectuals surrounded by books in Greek and Hebrew, pondering meanings too deep for ordinary people. The method of Bible study that has been popular for some time focuses on the strangeness of the Bible. It was written long ago, far away, and in languages we cannot read. There is a huge gap between us and the original readers of the Bible, a gap that can only be bridged by scholars, not by average folk.

There is some truth and some value in that "scholarly" method. It is true that the Bible was not written originally to us. Knowing ancient languages and customs can at times help us understand the Bible better. However, one unintended result of this approach is to make the Bible distant from the people of God. We may come to think that we can only hear God indirectly through Scripture, that his Word must be filtered through scholars. We may even think deep Bible study is a matter of mastering obscure information about the Bible.

Meditation

But we read the Bible for more than information. By studying it, we experience transformation, the mysterious process of God at work in us. Through his loving words, God is calling us to life with him. He is forming us into the image of his Son.

Reading the Bible is not like reading other books. We are not simply trying to learn information or master material. Instead, we want to stand under the authority of Scripture and let God master us. While we read the Bible, it reads us, opening the depths of our being to the overpowering love of God. "For the word of God is alive and active. Sharper than any double-edged sword, it penetrates even to dividing soul and spirit, joints and marrow; it judges the thoughts and attitudes of the heart. Nothing in all creation is hidden from God's sight. Everything is uncovered and laid bare before the eyes of him to whom we must give account" (Heb. 4:12–13 NIV).

Opening our hearts to the Word of God is meditation. Although this way of reading the Bible may be new to some, it has a long heritage among God's people. The psalmist joyously meditates on the words of God (Ps. 1:2; 39:3; 119:15, 23, 27, 48, 78, 97, 99, 148). Meditation is taking the words of Scripture to heart and letting them ask questions of us. It is slowing down, chewing over a text, listening closely, reading God's message of love to us over and over. This is not a simple, easy, or naïve reading of Scripture, but a process that takes time, dedication, and practice on our part.

There are many ways to meditate on the Bible. One is praying the Scriptures. Prayer and Bible study cannot be separated. One way of praying the Bible is to make the words of a text your prayer. Obviously, the prayer texts of Scripture, especially the Psalms, lend themselves to this. "The Lord is my shepherd" has been the prayer of many hearts.

However, it is proper and helpful to turn the words of the Bible into prayers. Commands from God can become prayers. "You shall have no other gods before me" (Exod. 20:3 NIV) can be prayed: "Lord, keep me from anything that takes your place in my heart." Stories can be prayed. Jesus heals a man born blind (John 9), and so we pray, "Lord Jesus, open my eyes to who you truly are." Even the promises of the Bible become prayers. "Never will I leave you; never will I forsake you" (Deut. 31:6; Heb. 13:5 NIV) becomes, "God, help me know your promise that you are always with me so I may live my life without fear."

Obviously, there are many helpful ways of hearing the voice of God in Scripture. Again, the purpose of Bible reading and study is not to know more about the Bible, much less to pride ourselves as experts on Scripture; instead, we read to hear the voice of our Beloved—we listen for a word of God for us.

Holy Reading

This commentary reflects one ancient way of meditation and praying the Scriptures known as *lectio divina*, or holy reading. This method assumes God wants to speak to us directly in the Bible, that the passage we are reading is God's Word to us right now. The writers of the New Testament read the Old Testament with this same conviction. They saw the words of the Bible speaking directly to their own situations. They read with humility and with prayer.

The first step along this way of holy reading is listening to the Bible. Choose a biblical text that is not too long. This commentary breaks most chapters into smaller sections. It is helpful to hear the Bible in different translations. The passages in this commentary from Proverbs are from the New International Version, those from Ecclesiastes are from the New Living Translation, and those from Job are from the English Standard Version. *Note that this book will not look at every verse in these books of the Bible.* You may not find a meditation here on your favorite verse. The purpose is to hear God's voice in your current situation, not to cover material or prepare lessons. Get into a comfortable position and maintain silence before God for several minutes. This prepares the heart to listen. Read slowly. Savor each word. Perhaps read aloud. Listen for a particular phrase that speaks to you. Ask God, What are you trying to tell me today?

The next step is to meditate on that phrase. That meditation may include slowly repeating the phrase that seems to be for you today. As you think deeply on it, you might even memorize it. Committing biblical passages to memory allows us to hold them in our hearts all day long. If you keep a journal, you might write the passage there. Let those words sink deeply into your heart.

Then pray those words back to God in your heart. Those words may call up visual images, smells, sounds, and feelings. Pay attention to what God is giving you in those words. Then respond in faith to what those words say to your heart. What do they call you to be and to do? Our humble response might take the form of praise, thanksgiving, joy, confession, or even cries of pain.

The final step in this "holy reading" is contemplation of God. The words from God that we receive deeply in our hearts lead us to him. Through these words, we experience union with the all-powerful God of love. Again, one should not separate Bible reading from prayer. The words of God in Scripture transport us into the very presence of God where we joyfully rest in his love.

What keeps us from reading our own desires back into Scripture? How do we know it is God's voice we hear and not our own?

Two things. One is prayer. We are asking God to open our hearts, minds, and lives to him. We ask to hear his voice, not ours and not the voice of the world around us.

The second thing that keeps this from being an exercise in self-deception is to study the Bible in community. By praying over Scripture in a group, we hear God's Word together. God speaks through the other members of our group. The wisdom he gives them keeps us from private, selfish, and unusual interpretations. They help us keep our own voices in check as we desire to listen to God alone.

How to Use This Commentary

This commentary assists us in holy reading of the Bible. It gives structure to daily personal devotions, family meditation, small group Bible studies, and church classes.

Daily Devotional

Listening, meditation, prayer, contemplation. How does this commentary fit into this way of Bible study? Consider it as a conversation partner. We have taken a section of Scripture and then broken it down into four short daily readings. After listening, meditating, praying, and contemplating the passage for the day, use the questions suggested in the commentary to provoke deeper reflection. This provides a structure for a daily fifteen-minute devotional four days a week. On the fifth day, read the entire passage, meditate, and then use the questions to reflect on the meaning of the whole scripture. On day six, explore a series of meditations on the passage, which you can treat like conversation with another who has prayed over the text.

If you want to begin daily Bible reading but need guidance, this provides a Monday through Saturday experience that prepares the heart for worship and praise on Sunday. This structure also results in a communal reading of Scripture, instead of a private reading. Even if you use this commentary alone, you are not reading privately. God is at work in you and in the conversation you have with another (the author of the commentary) who has sought to hear God through this passage of the Bible.

Family Bible Study

This commentary can also provide a space for family Bible study. Many Christian parents want to lead their children in daily study but don't know where to begin or how to structure their time. Using the six-day plan outlined above means the entire family can read, meditate, pray, and reflect on the shorter passages, using the questions provided. On day five, your family can review the entire passage, and then on day six, read the meditations in the commentary to prompt reflection and discussion. God will bless our families beyond our imaginations through the prayerful study of his Word.

Weekly Group Study

This commentary can also structure small group Bible study. Each member of the group should have meditated over the daily readings and questions for the five days preceding the group meeting, using the method outlined above. The day before the group meeting, each member should read and reflect on the meditations in the commentary on that passage. You then can meet once a week to hear God's Word together. In that group meeting, the method of holy reading would look something like this:

Listening
1. Five minutes of silence
2. Slow reading of the biblical passage for that week
3. A minute of silent meditation on the passage
4. Brief sharing with the group the word or phrase that struck you

Personal Message
5. A second reading of the same passage
6. A minute of silence
7. Where does this touch your life today?
8. Responses: I hear, I see, etc.

Life Response
9. Brief silence
10. What does God want you to do today in light of this word?

Group Prayer
11. Have each member of the group pray aloud for the person on his or her left, asking God to bless the word he has given them.

The procedure suggested here can be used in churches or neighborhood Bible studies. Church members would use the daily readings Monday to Friday in their daily devotionals. This commentary intentionally provides no readings on the sixth day so we can spend Saturdays as a time of rest—not rest from Bible study, but a time to let God's Word quietly work its way deep into our hearts. Sunday during Bible school or in-home meetings, the group would meet to experience the weekly readings together, using the group method described above. It might be that the sermon for each Sunday could be on the passage for that week.

Some churches have used this structure to great advantage. In the hallways of those church buildings, the talk is not of the local football team or the weather, but of the shared experience of the Word of God for that week. And that is the purpose of our personal and communal study—to hear the voice of God, our loving Father who wants us to love him in return. He deeply desires a personal relationship with us. Father, Son, and Spirit make a home inside us (see John 14:16–17, 23). Our loving God speaks to his children! But we must listen for his voice. That listening is not a matter of gritting our teeth and trying harder to hear. Instead, it is part of our entire life with God. That is what Bible study is all about.

Through daily personal prayer and meditation on God's Word and through a communal reading of Scripture, our most important conversation partner, the Holy Spirit, will do mysterious and marvelous work. Among other things, the Spirit pours God's love into our hearts (Rom. 5:5), bears witness to our spirits that we are God's children (Rom. 8:16), intercedes for us with God (Rom. 8:26), and enlightens us as to God's will (Eph. 1:17).

So this is an invitation to personal daily Bible study, to praying the Scriptures, to sharing with fellow believers, to hearing the voice of God. God will bless us, our families, our churches, and his world if we take the time to be still, listen, and do his word.

Introduction

THE SPIRITUALITY OF PROVERBS, ECCLESIASTES, AND JOB

These books are known as the Wisdom books because more than 50 percent of the uses of the word "wisdom" in the Old Testament are found in these books. What is "wisdom" in the Bible? The word usually refers less to factual knowledge and more to skill. It is more "know how" than "know that." The first time "wisdom" is used in the Old Testament, it refers to those who are skilled in making priestly clothing or the furnishings of the tabernacle (see Exod. 28:3; 31:6). Then the word was used to speak of those who were skilled in living. Biblical wisdom deals with knowing how to live.

"Wisdom," then, has to do with moral living. In the Old Testament, ethical instruction takes several forms. One finds it in the legal material of Exodus, Leviticus, and Deuteronomy. It is imbedded in the narratives of Genesis and the historical books. Prophetic oracles many times contain ethical instruction. But the Old Testament wisdom books—Proverbs, Ecclesiastes, and Job—are the primary depositories of ethical instruction. That instruction takes the form of proverbs, story, and dialogue. It is more than "common sense" moral teaching but is always in the context of the fear of the Lord.

The Spirituality of Proverbs

A proverb is a traditional saying, passed down from earlier generations. Proverbs are didactic, optimistic, practical, and conservative. A proverb is a figure of speech. It is short, to the point, and by nature an oversimplification. Proverbs are not immutable laws. They are usually true, but not always. They are those things your mama and daddy taught you. "Eat your vegetables and you'll grow up big and strong," Mama said. But you ate your vegetables and grew up sickly. Was Mama wrong? No. Most of the time, her advice would be right and wise.

So biblical Proverbs are true (after all, they are in the Bible, God's Word to us). But they are true proverbially. We misunderstand them if we turn them into absolute truths.

The book of Proverbs is a collection of these proverbs on different themes. To help with meditation on them, this commentary groups the proverbs by theme. It does not follow "verse by verse." By meditating on these proverbs, we catch a glimpse of the God of creation, the God of order, and the loving Father who passes on wisdom to his children.

The Spirituality of Ecclesiastes

Ecclesiastes contains a different kind of wisdom. It is built on the wisdom of Proverbs, but asks, what happens when proverbial wisdom fails? Ecclesiastes looks at the mysteries of life. It is reflective, speculative, pessimistic, and creative. It asks the hard questions, like, how does life make sense? It answers, *Often, it doesn't.* Plans fail. Fools triumph.

But Ecclesiastes is in the Bible. It is there for a reason. It points us to a trust in God, a fear of the Lord, that goes beyond the limits of human reason. The writer of Ecclesiastes tries all the ways that promise meaning in life. In the end, he is left with God alone. Meditating on his reflections can open the way for a spirituality that goes beyond the traditional.

The Spirituality of Job

That deeper spirituality is put to the test in Job. Job raises this deeply human question: How do we explain the ways of God in the face of the suffering of the innocent? Job is destroyed by the Lord through no fault of his own. Job continues to maintain his innocence, even though his friends repeatedly try to convince him he has deserved the disasters he has experienced. Job constantly wants an answer from God. But the only answer he gets is the presence of the Lord himself.

"The fear of the Lord is the beginning of wisdom." This is a repeated theme in Proverbs. Job experiences a deeper fear of the Lord, one based on trust alone. By meditating on the ordeal of Job, we are brought closer to a God we might not like and do not understand. The only God we have.

MEDITATIONS

PROVERBS
PASSAGES FROM THE NEW INTERNATIONAL VERSION

THE VALUE OF WISDOM
1:1–19

DAY ONE READING AND QUESTIONS

The proverbs of Solomon son of David, king of Israel:
for gaining wisdom and instruction;
    for understanding words of insight;
for receiving instruction in prudent behavior,
    doing what is right and just and fair;
for giving prudence to those who are simple,
    knowledge and discretion to the young— (1:1–4)

1. Why is Proverbs particularly associated with Solomon?

2. What are the similarities and differences between wisdom, instruction, insight, knowledge, prudence, and discretion?

3. Why do the simple and the young particularly need wisdom?

DAY TWO READING AND QUESTIONS

let the wise listen and add to their learning,
    and let the discerning get guidance—
for understanding proverbs and parables,
    the sayings and riddles of the wise.
The fear of the Lord is the beginning of knowledge,
    but fools despise wisdom and instruction. (1:5–7)

1. Why do the wise and discerning still need learning and guidance?

2. How does listening relate to wisdom? What does it mean to listen?

3. What is the fear of the Lord? How does it relate to wisdom?

DAY THREE READING AND QUESTIONS

Listen, my son, to your father's instruction
    and do not forsake your mother's teaching.
They are a garland to grace your head
    and a chain to adorn your neck.
My son, if sinful men entice you,
    do not give in to them.
If they say, "Come along with us;
    let's lie in wait for innocent blood,
    let's ambush some harmless soul;
let's swallow them alive, like the grave,
    and whole, like those who go down to the pit;
we will get all sorts of valuable things
    and fill our houses with plunder;
cast lots with us;
    we will all share the loot"— (1:8–14)

1. Who are the teachers of wisdom in these verses? Why are those teachers so important?

2. What does it mean to be enticed? How do others entice us?

3. What particular sin or foolishness is mentioned here? Why might some find that enticing?

DAY FOUR READING AND QUESTIONS

> my son, do not go along with them,
>   do not set foot on their paths;
> for their feet rush into evil,
>   they are swift to shed blood.
> How useless to spread a net
>   where every bird can see it!
> These men lie in wait for their own blood;
>   they ambush only themselves!
> Such are the paths of all who go after ill-gotten gain;
>   it takes away the life of those who get it. (1:15–19)

1. What is the role of feet in this passage? Why is it important where you put your feet?

2. What happens to those who plan to violently hurt others?

3. What is the relationship between wisdom and life?

DAY FIVE READING AND QUESTIONS

Go back and read Proverbs 1:1–19.

1. Do people today often talk about wisdom? Why or why not?

2. What has taken the place of wisdom in our culture?

3. What are the ways God gives wisdom in this passage?

Meditation on the Value of Wisdom (1:1–19)

We do not know how to live when we are born. We have to be taught.

Usually, our parents are our first teachers. They teach us so many things—how to walk, eat, and tie our shoes. How to tell time. How to read and write.

More importantly, good parents teach us skills for living. They teach us how to be skilled in life itself—what actions lead to life, what actions lead to death. The Bible uses many words for being skilled in living: wisdom, instruction, insight, knowledge, prudence, discretion.

Parents teach what they were taught, truths that stand the tests of time. Those teachings are contained in short, pithy sayings known as proverbs. Our parents might be our first teachers, but they are not our only teachers. Earlier generations guide us through proverbs.

The ancient sayings in the book of Proverbs may sound strange to us. Our culture has largely lost the word "wisdom" and replaced it with information or data. But Proverbs reminds us that we still need to be skilled in living. We must learn from those who went before us.

These first words of Proverbs show us the two things that are necessary to be wise. We must listen. Listen to the teachings of wise fathers and mothers. But most importantly, we must listen to the Lord. "The fear of the Lord is the beginning of knowledge." The wisdom of Proverbs is not merely human wisdom. It is the gift of the all-wise God.

"God who made us, teach us how to live."

CHARACTERISTICS OF WISDOM
Humility

DAY ONE READING AND QUESTIONS

To fear the Lord is to hate evil;
    I hate pride and arrogance,
        evil behavior and perverse speech. (8:13)

When pride comes, then comes disgrace,
    but with humility comes wisdom. (11:2)

Where there is strife, there is pride,
    but wisdom is found in those who take advice. (13:10)

1. What does it mean to hate pride? Do we always think of pride as evil?

2. How can pride lead to disgrace?

3. Why does strife often lead to pride?

DAY TWO READING AND QUESTIONS

The Lord tears down the house of the proud,
    but he sets the widow's boundary stones in place. (15:25)

Wisdom's instruction is to fear the Lord,
    and humility comes before honor. (15:33)

The Lord detests all the proud of heart.
    Be sure of this: They will not go unpunished. (16:5)

1. Why is pride contrasted with being a widow? What was it like to be a widow in biblical times?

2. How can humility lead to honor? Are we not proud when we receive honor?

3. What are some examples of God punishing the proud?

DAY THREE READING AND QUESTIONS

Pride goes before destruction,
>   a haughty spirit before a fall.
Better to be lowly in spirit along with the oppressed
>   than to share plunder with the proud. (16:18–19)

Before a downfall the heart is haughty,
>   but humility comes before honor. (18:12)

Haughty eyes and a proud heart—
>   the unplowed field of the wicked—produce sin. (21:4)

1. What does "haughty" mean? How is it related to pride?

2. How are the proud contrasted with the oppressed?

3. How is pride connected to the eyes? What do haughty eyes look like?

DAY FOUR READING AND QUESTIONS

The proud and arrogant person—"Mocker" is his name—
>   behaves with insolent fury. (21:24)

It is not good to eat too much honey,
> nor is it honorable to search out matters that are too deep.
> (25:27)

Pride brings a person low,
> but the lowly in spirit gain honor. (29:23)

1. What does it mean to be a mocker? How does mocking show pride?

2. Do we sometimes pretend to know what we do not know? How is that pride?

3. How do pride and arrogance lead to anger?

DAY FIVE READING AND QUESTIONS

Go back and read all these verses.

1. Why do you think Proverbs speaks more often about pride than about humility?

2. What is humility? What are the results of humility in these verses?

3. What is the relationship of pride to injustice in these verses?

Meditation on Pride, Humility, and Wisdom

Pride. It's easier to see in others than in ourselves. We know it when we see it. The superior sneer. The cutting remark. We see it when every gesture screams, "I am better than you."

And the pride of others does more than hurt our feelings. Pride leads to the feelings of entitlement that allow people to neglect and cheat others with no guilty conscience. The proud take because it is their right. They cheat because they can.

God hates pride. That may make us feel good when we see pride in others; but what of our own pride? Our own pride is very hard for us to see. By definition, pride makes us blind to how we think we are better, smarter, and deserve more than others.

Pride ends with destruction. Wisdom calls instead for humility. While pride is easy to see in others, humility is hard to see. In our culture (perhaps in all cultures) humility is associated with weakness and powerlessness. Only those who are less valuable are humble.

But true wisdom from God turns those cultural values upside down. It is the all-powerful God, the one who deserves all honor, who protects the widows, the poor, the downtrodden, the humble.

Humility then comes from and leads to wisdom because it is an act of faith. We know we have value because we are children of God, not because we mistakenly think ourselves superior to others. And we know everyone we meet has that same value from God. Humility demands that we work for justice because our God is just.

"God of honor, honor us with humility and remove our pride."

CHARACTERISTICS OF WISDOM
Honesty

DAY ONE READING AND QUESTIONS

Honest Speech

Keep your mouth free of perversity;
　　Keep corrupt talk far from your lips. (4:24)

Truthful lips endure forever,
　　but a lying tongue lasts only a moment. (12:19)

Kings take pleasure in honest lips;
　　they value the one who speaks what is right. (16:13)

1. What are some examples of perverse talk and corrupt speech?

2. Why do lies last only a moment? If lies are quickly exposed, why do people lie?

3. Do leaders always love those who speak honestly? Why would they love honest speech?

DAY TWO READING AND QUESTIONS

Honesty in Business

The LORD detests dishonest scales,
　　but accurate weights find favor with him. (11:1)

Honest scales and balances belong to the LORD;
　　all the weights in the bag are of his making. (16:11)

Whoever walks in integrity walks securely,
> but whoever takes crooked paths will be found out. (10:9)

1. What is the contemporary equivalent to honest weights?

2. What should God's people charge for what they sell?

3. What is integrity? How does it keep one safe?

DAY THREE READING AND QUESTIONS

Honesty in Court

An honest witness tells the truth,
> but a false witness tells lies. (12:17)

An honest witness does not deceive,
> but a false witness pours out lies. (14:5)

A truthful witness saves lives,
> but a false witness is deceitful. (14:25)

1. Why is it so important to be truthful as a witness?

2. Why would one lie as a witness?

3. How can a truthful witness save lives?

DAY FOUR READING AND QUESTIONS

Honesty with Others and with God

An honest answer
> is like a kiss on the lips. (24:26)

Better is open rebuke
    than hidden love. (27:5)

Whoever rebukes a person will in the end gain favor
    rather than one who has a flattering tongue. (28:23)

Whoever conceals their sins does not prosper,
    but the one who confesses and renounces them finds mercy. (28:13)

1. Do you appreciate honest criticism?

2. Why are we sometimes reluctant to give criticism or rebuke?

3. Should we try to conceal our sins from God? Should we try to conceal our sins from others?

DAY FIVE READING AND QUESTIONS

Go back and read all these verses.

1. Can one teach and learn honesty? How does that work?

2. What are some consequences of dishonesty?

3. If honesty is the best policy, why is there so much dishonesty?

Meditation on Honesty and Wisdom

"Honesty is the best policy."

    That's not a quote from the Bible, but it summarizes what Proverbs says about honesty. If we are honest in our speech, we won't get caught in a lie. If we give fair goods and services for fair prices, our business will prosper. If we are honest in court, justice will prevail. If we are honest with our friends, even if that honesty includes criticism, our friendship will be deep. If we are honest to God, he will forgive.

So, if honesty is the best policy, why is there so much dishonesty? Why do we often lie, or at least shade the truth?

The answer from Proverbs is, we lie because we are fools. "Fools" in Proverbs refers not to those of low intelligence but to those who should know better and still choose the wrong path. We lie and become fools because we have been deceived into thinking lies will help us. We think we will not be found out, that we can get away with lies. But Proverbs says (and we know it is true deep in our hearts) lies will always hurt.

So, if honesty is the best policy, can we learn to be honest? At first, it may seem we cannot. Honesty is a matter of character. There are no tips or shortcuts to being honest.

But we can remind ourselves, as these proverbs remind us, that the path of honesty leads to prosperity, justice, and right relationship with others and with God. We need those reminders to keep us from foolish deception.

"God of truth, make us honest in our words and deeds."

CHARACTERISTICS OF WISDOM
Diligence in Work

DAY ONE READING AND QUESTIONS

Go to the ant, you sluggard;
>consider its ways and be wise!

It has no commander,
>no overseer or ruler,

yet it stores its provisions in summer
>and gathers its food at harvest.

How long will you lie there, you sluggard?
>When will you get up from your sleep?

A little sleep, a little slumber,
>a little folding of the hands to rest—

and poverty will come on you like a thief
>and scarcity like an armed man. (6:6–11)

1. How are we urged to be like ants in these verses?

2. Why is sleep condemned in this passage? Is it wrong to sleep?

3. What does the ant get for its work? What happens to the sluggard?

DAY TWO READING AND QUESTIONS

Lazy hands make for poverty,
>but diligent hands bring wealth.

He who gathers crops in summer is a prudent son,
>but he who sleeps during harvest is a disgraceful son. (10:4–5)

Those who work their land will have abundant food,
> but those who chase fantasies have no sense. (12:11)

From the fruit of their lips people are filled with good things,
> and the work of their hands brings them reward. (12:14)

Diligent hands will rule,
> but laziness ends in forced labor. (12:24)

The lazy do not roast any game,
> but the diligent feed on the riches of the hunt. (12:27)

1. What blessings come from work in these verses?

2. What are the results of laziness in these verses?

3. What does it mean to "chase fantasies"? How does this relate to laziness?

DAY THREE READING AND QUESTIONS

A sluggard's appetite is never filled,
> but the desires of the diligent are fully satisfied. (13:4)

Hard work brings a profit,
> but mere talk leads only to poverty. (14:23)

The appetite of laborers works for them;
> their hunger drives them on. (16:26)

One who is slack in his work
> is brother to one who destroys. (18:9)

Do not love sleep or you will grow poor;
> stay awake and you will have food to spare. (20:13)

The craving of a sluggard will be the death of him,
> because his hands refuse to work. (21:25)

1. Does hard work always lead to prosperity?

2. Is the profit motive a good thing or a bad thing?

3. How is laziness destructive?

DAY FOUR READING AND QUESTIONS

Do you see someone skilled in their work?
> They will serve before kings;
> they will not serve before officials of low rank. (22:29)

Do not wear yourself out to get rich;
> do not trust your own cleverness.
Cast but a glance at riches, and they are gone,
> for they will surely sprout wings
> and fly off to the sky like an eagle. (23:4–5)

I went past the field of a sluggard,
> past the vineyard of someone who has no sense;
thorns had come up everywhere,
> the ground was covered with weeds,
> and the stone wall was in ruins.
I applied my heart to what I observed
> and learned a lesson from what I saw:
A little sleep, a little slumber,
> a little folding of the hands to rest—
and poverty will come on you like a thief
> and scarcity like an armed man. (24:30–34)

Those who work their land will have abundant food,
>   but those who chase fantasies will have their fill of poverty. (28:19)

1. If work brings profit and prosperity, why are there warnings here about wealth and riches?

2. How does the state of one's property reflect hard work or laziness?

3. Why are there so few competent workers?

DAY FIVE READING AND QUESTIONS

Go back and read all these verses.

1. If laziness brings ruin, why are so many people lazy?

2. Can one work too hard? If so, what would that look like?

3. Do you see yourself as a hard worker or as a lazy person?

Meditation on Diligence in Work

"Give an honest day's work for an honest day's pay."

"Don't work too hard."

I grew up hearing both phrases from my parents. And even though they seem to contradict, I don't think they do. Instead, they seem to reflect what Proverbs says about work.

One should give an honest day's work. Hard work brings profit and prosperity. It gives one the respect of others.

On the other hand, if one is lazy, poverty, hunger, and shame will follow.

However, there are limits to the value of work. One can work "too hard" if that work leads to greed for wealth, position, and power. Work can blind one to what is truly important: relationship with God, family, and others. It can lead to burnout. "Don't wear yourself out trying to get rich. Be wise enough to know when to quit." God commands rest ("Remember the Sabbath") as well as work.

So, remember that Proverbs is part of the Bible—that is, it is in the context of the relationship and covenant God has with us. So we pray, "Give us this day our daily bread," knowing we depend on God for everything. Yet that bread also comes as a result of hard work.

Do not be lazy. Work hard. But work with and for the Lord.

"God who gives all good gifts, give us the gift of diligence in our work."

CHARACTERISTICS OF WISDOM
Wise Speech

DAY ONE READING AND QUESTIONS

Wisdom is found on the lips of the discerning,
  but a rod is for the back of one who has no sense.
The wise store up knowledge,
  but the mouth of a fool invites ruin. (10:13–14)

Sin is not ended by multiplying words,
  but the prudent hold their tongues.
The tongue of the righteous is choice silver,
  but the heart of the wicked is of little value.
The lips of the righteous nourish many,
  but fools die for lack of sense. (10:19–21)

1. How are discernment and prudence related to speech?

2. How is the tongue related to the heart?

3. What does it mean for "lips to nourish many"? How do words feed others?

DAY TWO READING AND QUESTIONS

The words of the reckless pierce like swords,
  but the tongue of the wise brings healing.
Truthful lips endure forever,
  but a lying tongue lasts only a moment. (12:18–19)

The tongue of the wise adorns knowledge,
> but the mouth of the fool gushes folly.
The eyes of the LORD are everywhere,
> keeping watch on the wicked and the good.
The soothing tongue is a tree of life,
> but a perverse tongue crushes the spirit. (15:2–4)

1. What blessings come from the lips and the tongue in these verses?

2. What evil comes from the lips and the tongue in these verses?

3. Why does lying not last?

DAY THREE READING AND QUESTIONS

A wicked person listens to deceitful lips;
> a liar pays attention to a destructive tongue.
Whoever mocks the poor shows contempt for their Maker;
> whoever gloats over disaster will not go unpunished. (17:4–5)

One whose heart is corrupt does not prosper;
> one whose tongue is perverse falls into trouble. (17:20)

The one who has knowledge uses words with restraint,
> and whoever has understanding is even-tempered.
Even fools are thought wise if they keep silent,
> and discerning if they hold their tongues. (17:27–28)

1. What part does listening play in these verses?

2. What do mocking and gloating have to do with speech?

3. What is the value of silence?

DAY FOUR READING AND QUESTIONS

A fortune made by a lying tongue
    is a fleeting vapor and a deadly snare. (21:6)

Those who guard their mouths and their tongues
    keep themselves from calamity. (21:23)

Through patience a ruler can be persuaded,
    and a gentle tongue can break a bone. (25:15)

Like a club or a sword or a sharp arrow
    is one who gives false testimony against a neighbor. (25:18)

Like a north wind that brings unexpected rain
    is a sly tongue—which provokes a horrified look. (25:23)

1. How does speech relate to prosperity?

2. How powerful is the tongue in helping or harming others?

3. What is a "sly tongue"? Why would words from a sly tongue bring a horrified look?

DAY FIVE READING AND QUESTIONS

Go back and read all these verses.

1. If one is thinking bad thoughts, why shouldn't one speak those thoughts?

2. If you do not tell others what you are thinking, are you being honest with them?

3. Why is it so hard to speak less?

Meditation on Wise Speech

"Sticks and stones may break my bones, but words will never harm me."

I grew up with this proverb. But the book of Proverbs has the opposite teaching. Words can do great harm, worse than broken bones. And our experience bears that out. Years later, we may barely remember a beating, but we still hurt from words spoken long ago. Those hurtful words sink deeply into our bones.

"Think before you speak."

I also heard this in my childhood. It clearly summarizes what Proverbs says. But thinking before speaking is much harder than it sounds. We blurt out hurtful thoughts before we know it.

But shouldn't we always be honest in our speech? Shouldn't we always tell what we are thinking? Our culture prizes candor and frankness. Social media, "reality" television, and tell-all books model the practice of saying whatever comes into our heads with no thought of consequences.

Proverbs calls this foolish speech. And foolish speech leads to poverty, hatred, and even violence.

Wise speech is less speech. Sometimes (many times) the best thing to say is nothing. "If you have nothing good to say, then say nothing at all." Wise speech is thoughtful speech. We wait to speak until we have deliberated on how best to say things. Wise speech is helpful, gracious, and kind.

So, when do we speak, and when are we silent? And when we speak, what words do we use? The best rule for speech (and one that reflects the teaching of Proverbs) is this: speak only what love requires.

Speak only what love requires. That means we speak out of love, not anger or quick reaction. It means we take time to weigh the impact of our words. We ask, will my words help this person or situation? If not, we do not speak.

"God of love, slow down my tongue this day, so I may speak only what love requires."

CHARACTERISTICS OF WISDOM
Wealth, Poverty, and Justice

DAY ONE READING AND QUESTIONS

The Value of Riches

The wealth of the rich is their fortified city,
  but poverty is the ruin of the poor. (10:15)

A person's riches may ransom their life,
  but the poor cannot respond to threatening rebukes. (13:8)

The poor are shunned even by their neighbors,
  but the rich have many friends. (14:20)

The poor are shunned by all their relatives—
  how much more do their friends avoid them!

Though the poor pursue them with pleading,
  they are nowhere to be found. (19:7)

The rich rule over the poor,
  and the borrower is slave to the lender. (22:7)

1. What are the advantages to wealth in these verses?

2. What are the disadvantages of poverty in these passages?

3. Given the choice, would you rather be rich than poor? Why?

DAY TWO READING AND QUESTIONS

The Limits of Wealth and Poverty

Such are the paths of all who go after ill-gotten gain;
    it takes away the life of those who get it. (1:19)

One person pretends to be rich, yet has nothing;
    another pretends to be poor, yet has great wealth. (13:7)

An unplowed field produces food for the poor,
    but injustice sweeps it away. (13:23)

Better a little with the fear of the LORD
    than great wealth with turmoil. (15:16)

The greedy bring ruin to their households,
    but the one who hates bribes will live. (15:27)

Better a little with righteousness
    than much gain with injustice. (16:8)

1. What are the dangers of riches in these verses?

2. What does it mean to be greedy? Is it easy to see greed in others? Is it easy to see it in ourselves?

3. Why would wealth bring turmoil? Isn't wealth supposed to bring peace of mind?

DAY THREE READING AND QUESTIONS

Wealth and Justice

The wicked accept bribes in secret
    to pervert the course of justice. (17:23)

The poor plead for mercy,
>   but the rich answer harshly. (18:23)

One who oppresses the poor to increase his wealth
>   and one who gives gifts to the rich—both come to poverty. (22:16)

Do not exploit the poor because they are poor
>   and do not crush the needy in court,
for the Lord will take up their case
>   and will exact life for life. (22:22–23)

Do not move an ancient boundary stone
>   or encroach on the fields of the fatherless,
for their Defender is strong;
>   he will take up their case against you. (23:10–11)

A ruler who oppresses the poor
>   is like a driving rain that leaves no crops. (28:3)

Whoever increases wealth by taking interest or profit from the poor
>   amasses it for another, who will be kind to the poor. (28:8)

The righteous care about justice for the poor,
>   but the wicked have no such concern. (29:7)

1. *What are some specific ways the rich exploit the poor in these verses?*

2. *What does it mean to move a boundary stone? What is the contemporary equivalent to this? Why is it so wrong?*

3. *Who defends the poor?*

DAY FOUR READING AND QUESTIONS

Wisdom Is Greater than Wealth

How much better to get wisdom than gold,
  to get insight rather than silver! (16:16)

Better to be lowly in spirit along with the oppressed
  than to share plunder with the proud. (16:19)

Better the poor whose walk is blameless
  than a fool whose lips are perverse. (19:1)

The rich are wise in their own eyes;
  one who is poor and discerning sees how deluded they are. (28:11)

Rich and poor have this in common:
  The LORD is the Maker of them all. (22:2)

1. Why is wisdom greater than riches?

2. How do riches easily deceive and delude those who have them?

3. Why is it important to remember that God made both rich and poor? How does this make rich and poor the same?

DAY FIVE READING AND QUESTIONS

Go back and read all these verses on wealth, poverty, and justice.

1. Why do Proverbs and the rest of the Bible talk so often on money?

2. Do contemporary Christians and churches talk too often or too little about money? What is the message on money in your church?

3. What does justice look like in the Bible?

Meditation on Wealth, Poverty, and Justice

"It's money that matters."

So goes the song from Randy Newman. A song that was meant to be tongue in cheek.

"It's money that matters."

If we are honest, we must admit we think that way sometimes, perhaps much of the time. Even some of the proverbs sound that way. Money brings protection, power, and popularity.

But that is not the whole story, as Proverbs also reminds us. Money usually leads to greed, which in turn brings pretense, turmoil, ruin, and death. Worst of all, money easily comes from and leads to injustice. We make our money directly or indirectly on the backs of the poor. Intentionally or thoughtlessly, we profit from the poor, cheat the powerless, and exploit the worker. Even "good" people do this because we do not care about justice for the poor. We assume the economic system is fair to all.

But God defends the poor. And if we prize wisdom above money and comfort, then we are on the side of the Lord. The side of the poor. We know who gives us our daily bread, so we share that gift with others.

"Defender of the poor, open our eyes to injustice. Keep us from thoughtless greed."

CHARACTERISTICS OF WISDOM
Family

DAY ONE READING AND QUESTIONS

Wisdom and Marriage

Drink water from your own cistern,
    running water from your own well.
Should your springs overflow in the streets,
    your streams of water in the public squares?
Let them be yours alone,
    never to be shared with strangers.
May your fountain be blessed,
    and may you rejoice in the wife of your youth. (5:15–18)

He who finds a wife finds what is good
    and receives favor from the Lord. (18:22)

Better to live on a corner of the roof
    than share a house with a quarrelsome wife. (21:9)

Better to live in a desert
    than with a quarrelsome and nagging wife. (21:19)

A wife of noble character who can find?
    She is worth far more than rubies.

Her husband has full confidence in her
    and lacks nothing of value. (31:10–11)

1. Why are these proverbs addressed to men?

2. Could the negative descriptions of wives here (quarrelsome and nagging) also apply to husbands?

3. What do these verses imply about the purposes of marriage?

DAY TWO READING AND QUESTIONS

Children as a Blessing

The proverbs of Solomon:
A wise son brings joy to his father,
    but a foolish son brings grief to his mother. (10:1)

A wise son heeds his father's instruction,
    but a mocker does not respond to rebukes. (13:1)

Whoever fears the LORD has a secure fortress,
    and for their children it will be a refuge. (14:26)

A wise son brings joy to his father,
    but a foolish man despises his mother. (15:20)

Children's children are a crown to the aged,
    and parents are the pride of their children. (17:6)

Listen to your father, who gave you life,
    and do not despise your mother when she is old.
Buy the truth and do not sell it—
    wisdom, instruction and insight as well.
The father of a righteous child has great joy;
    a man who fathers a wise son rejoices in him.
May your father and mother rejoice;
    may she who gave you birth be joyful! (23:22–25)

1. What does the wise son (child) do in these verses?

2. How are parents to be a refuge for their children?

3. What do truth, wisdom, instruction, and insight have to do with being a good child or a good parent?

DAY THREE READING AND QUESTIONS

Children as a Curse

To have a fool for a child brings grief;
    there is no joy for the parent of a godless fool. (17:21)

A foolish son brings grief to his father
    and bitterness to the mother who bore him. (17:25)

Whoever robs their father and drives out their mother
    is a child who brings shame and disgrace. (19:26)

If someone curses their father or mother,
    their lamp will be snuffed out in pitch darkness. (20:20)

A discerning son heeds instruction,
    but a companion of gluttons disgraces his father. (28:7)

Whoever robs their father or mother
    and says, "It's not wrong,"
    is partner to one who destroys. (28:24)

1. What are the ways children harm their parents in these verses?

2. What are some ways children rob their parents?

3. What makes a child a fool in these verses?

DAY FOUR READING AND QUESTIONS

Wisdom and Discipline

Whoever spares the rod hates their children,
> but the one who loves their children is careful to discipline them. (13:24)

Even small children are known by their actions,
> so is their conduct really pure and upright? (20:11)

Start children off on the way they should go,
> and even when they are old they will not turn from it. (22:6)

Do not withhold discipline from a child;
> if you punish them with the rod, they will not die.

Punish them with the rod
> and save them from death. (23:13–14)

A rod and a reprimand impart wisdom,
> but a child left undisciplined disgraces its mother. (29:15)

Discipline your children, and they will give you peace;
> they will bring you the delights you desire. (29:17)

1. Are we required to discipline our children with a rod? What are other ways of discipline?

2. What is the difference between discipline and punishment?

3. Why should parents discipline their children?

DAY FIVE READING AND QUESTIONS

Go back and read all these verses on family.

1. What are some of the joys of marriage?

2. What are some of the joys of children?

3. What are some of the challenges of children?

Meditation on Family

These proverbs are some of the most offensive to our sensibilities. They seem at first glance to paint most women as quarrelsome and nagging. Children should be beaten often with the rod to raise them right. These sound like the stereotypes of a time gone by, a time we are glad to see gone.

But with a closer look, we can see the wisdom behind these offensive sayings. Proverbs is addressed directly to "sons"; hence, the warnings against spreading "water" promiscuously are a clear call to sexual faithfulness in marriage. Such a call would certainly also apply to women.

The warning against marrying someone who is quarrelsome and nagging applies to men also (surely we have all met quarrelsome and nagging men). Behind this counsel is the implied wisdom of taking the time to know someone's character before getting married.

Even the many proverbs on the rod reflect the grave responsibilities of parents to train and discipline their children. Many parents believe corporal punishment is not the best way to discipline, which requires them to be creative and appropriate in their punishment and discipline of their children.

Parents have a grave responsibility for disciplining their children, but they are not completely responsible for them. Children, especially grown children, have freewill and responsibility. I think the most misunderstood proverb in the years I was growing up was, "Start children off on the way they should go, and even when they are old they will not turn from it" (22:6). Many thought of this as an absolute saying. As a result, they completely blamed themselves when their adult children did evil. But like all proverbs, this statement is *usually* true. It meant to encourage good parenting, not promote needless guilt.

So even (maybe especially) proverbs that go against our sensibilities can teach us, if we have ears to hear.

"Father God, who disciplines his children out of love, give us wisdom as husbands, wives, parents, and children."

CHARACTERISTICS OF WISDOM
Friendship

DAY ONE READING AND QUESTIONS

False Friendship

Wealth attracts many friends,
> but even the closest friend of the poor person deserts them. (19:4)

Many curry favor with a ruler,
> and everyone is the friend of one who gives gifts. (19:6)

The poor are shunned by all their relatives—
> how much more do their friends avoid them!
Though the poor pursue them with pleading,
> they are nowhere to be found. (19:7)

1. What kind of friend is attracted by wealth?

2. Why does one want to be friends with a ruler or a gift giver? What kind of friendship is that?

3. Why do friends avoid the poor?

DAY TWO READING AND QUESTIONS

True Friendship

A friend loves at all times,
> and a brother is born for a time of adversity. (17:17)

One who has unreliable friends soon comes to ruin,
> but there is a friend who sticks closer than a brother. (18:24)

Many claim to have unfailing love,
> but a faithful person who can find? (20:6)

1. How is friendship tested in adversity?

2. Who are you closer to, family or friends? Why?

3. Is faithfulness the greatest characteristic of friendship? Why or why not?

DAY THREE READING AND QUESTIONS

Dangers to Friendship

A perverse person stirs up conflict,
> and a gossip separates close friends. (16:28)

Whoever would foster love covers over an offense,
> but whoever repeats the matter separates close friends. (17:9)

A gossip betrays a confidence;
> so avoid anyone who talks too much. (20:19)

Do not make friends with a hot-tempered person,
> do not associate with one easily angered,

or you may learn their ways
> and get yourself ensnared. (22:24–25)

1. How does gossip destroy friendship?

2. How do friends cover over offenses? How does this relate to honesty?

3. How does anger harm friendship?

DAY FOUR READING AND QUESTIONS

The Value of Friendship

Walk with the wise and become wise,
>for a companion of fools suffers harm. (13:20)

Wounds from a friend can be trusted,
but an enemy multiplies kisses. (27:6)

Perfume and incense bring joy to the heart,
>and the pleasantness of a friend
>>springs from their heartfelt advice.

Do not forsake your friend or a friend of your family,
>and do not go to your relative's house when disaster strikes you—
>better a neighbor nearby than a relative far away. (27:9–10)

As iron sharpens iron,
>so one person sharpens another. (27:17)

1. What benefits come from friendship according to these verses?

2. If someone wounds you with their words, can you still be their friend?

3. How do you get wisdom from your friends?

DAY FIVE READING AND QUESTIONS

Go back and read all these verses on wisdom and friendship.

1. What makes someone your friend?

2. Can one have too many friends? Why or why not?

3. What are the characteristics of true friendship?

Meditation on Wisdom and Friendship

There are friends and there are true friends. Today we suffer from friend inflation. When someone you don't even know can be your friend online with the click of a button, then "friend" has lost much of its meaning.

We know what it's like to have false friends. As Proverbs tells us, they are our friends when we have money or are influential and popular. False friends can lead us into anger and violence. They betray our secrets, stab us in the back, and break our hearts. As the song by Joan Jett and Kenny Laguna goes, "You don't lose when you lose fake friends."

By contrast, true friends make our lives immensely richer. True friends keep our confidences. They know us and love us so much that we can take and even welcome criticism from them. From them we gain wisdom.

Above all, true friends are loyal. They stick with us when everyone else avoids us. They are closer than family.

Just yesterday I had my weekly visit with four friends. We have met together for prayer each week for over twenty years. We've laughed, cried, confessed, griped, and argued. Most importantly, we have sought God's will together. They have sharpened me and made we wise. Of all the things I am thankful for, I thank God for friends.

"God of love, thank you for faithful companions along life's way."

WISDOM PERSONIFIED
Lady Wisdom—8:1–9:6

DAY ONE READING AND QUESTIONS

Does not wisdom call out?
    Does not understanding raise her voice?
At the highest point along the way,
    where the paths meet, she takes her stand;
beside the gate leading into the city,
    at the entrance, she cries aloud:
"To you, O people, I call out;
    I raise my voice to all mankind.
You who are simple, gain prudence;
    you who are foolish, set your hearts on it.
Listen, for I have trustworthy things to say;
    I open my lips to speak what is right.
My mouth speaks what is true,
    for my lips detest wickedness.
All the words of my mouth are just;
    none of them is crooked or perverse.
To the discerning all of them are right;
    they are upright to those who have found knowledge." (8:1–9)

1. *Why is it important that wisdom speaks at the crossroads and the city gate? Can everyone hear wisdom?*

2. *How does one learn from wisdom?*

3. *What does it mean to be crooked and perverse? How does this contrast with wisdom?*

DAY TWO READING AND QUESTIONS

"Choose my instruction instead of silver,
    knowledge rather than choice gold,
for wisdom is more precious than rubies,
    and nothing you desire can compare with her.
I, wisdom, dwell together with prudence;
    I possess knowledge and discretion.
To fear the Lord is to hate evil;
    I hate pride and arrogance,
    evil behavior and perverse speech.
Counsel and sound judgment are mine;
    I have insight, I have power.
By me kings reign
    and rulers issue decrees that are just;
by me princes govern,
    and nobles—all who rule on earth.
I love those who love me,
    and those who seek me find me.
With me are riches and honor,
    enduring wealth and prosperity.
My fruit is better than fine gold;
    what I yield surpasses choice silver.
I walk in the way of righteousness,
    along the paths of justice,
bestowing a rich inheritance on those who love me
    and making their treasuries full." (8:10–21)

1. Why is wisdom more valuable than silver, gold, or rubies?

2. How do kings reign through wisdom? What happens if rulers are not wise?

3. What are the results of wisdom in these verses?

DAY THREE READING AND QUESTIONS

"The LORD brought me forth as the first of his works,
    before his deeds of old;
I was formed long ages ago,
    at the very beginning, when the world came to be.
When there were no watery depths, I was given birth,
    when there were no springs overflowing with water;
before the mountains were settled in place,
    before the hills, I was given birth,
before he made the world or its fields
    or any of the dust of the earth.
I was there when he set the heavens in place,
    when he marked out the horizon on the face of the deep,
when he established the clouds above
    and fixed securely the fountains of the deep,
when he gave the sea its boundary
    so the waters would not overstep his command,
and when he marked out the foundations of the earth.
    Then I was constantly at his side.
I was filled with delight day after day,
    rejoicing always in his presence,
rejoicing in his whole world
    and delighting in mankind." (8:22–31)

1. Why is it significant that God created wisdom before anything else? What does that say about the importance of wisdom?

2. What was the role of wisdom in creation?

3. What does it mean that wisdom delighted in God, the world, and mankind?

DAY FOUR READING AND QUESTIONS

"Now then, my children, listen to me;
    blessed are those who keep my ways.
Listen to my instruction and be wise;
    do not disregard it.
Blessed are those who listen to me,
    watching daily at my doors,
    waiting at my doorway.
For those who find me find life
    and receive favor from the Lord.
But those who fail to find me harm themselves;
    all who hate me love death."
Wisdom has built her house;
    she has set up its seven pillars.
She has prepared her meat and mixed her wine;
    she has also set her table.
She has sent out her servants, and she calls
    from the highest point of the city,
    "Let all who are simple come to my house!"
To those who have no sense she says,
    "Come, eat my food
    and drink the wine I have mixed.
Leave your simple ways and you will live;
    walk in the way of insight." (8:32–9:6)

1. What does it mean to be a child of wisdom?

2. What does it mean to wait and watch for wisdom?

3. How is having wisdom like sharing a meal?

DAY FIVE READING AND QUESTIONS

Go back and read Proverbs 8:1–9:6

1. *Why is wisdom portrayed as a woman?*

2. *How is this portrait of wisdom similar to the description of the Word in John 1:1–5?*

3. *How important is wisdom in these verses?*

Meditation on Lady Wisdom (8:1–9:6)

"Welcome to my house!"

Who is this who invites us in? She was created before anything else. She assisted in creation and delighted in its goodness.

The owner of the house is lady wisdom. And what a house it is! Solid. Beautiful. Welcoming. And what a feast she has prepared for us—insight, instruction, and the favor of the Lord. And all are welcome. Wisdom sends her servants into the streets to invite everyone to the banquet.

And what are we asked to do? Listen to her invitation. Come to her house. Eat at her table. Eat all you want and be satisfied. Listen to her words that bring righteousness, honor, and life.

Wisdom gives free gifts. Wisdom herself is the great gift from the Lord. All we are asked to do is listen and receive.

"God who made wisdom, give us this gift today!"

A LIFETIME OF WISDOM
31:10–31

DAY ONE READING AND QUESTIONS

A wife of noble character who can find?
    She is worth far more than rubies.
Her husband has full confidence in her
    and lacks nothing of value.
She brings him good, not harm,
    all the days of her life.
She selects wool and flax
    and works with eager hands.
She is like the merchant ships,
    bringing her food from afar.
She gets up while it is still night;
    she provides food for her family
    and portions for her female servants. (31:10–15)

1. What does the woman do in these verses? Are these acts typically viewed as "women's work" in our society?

2. What does it look like for husbands to have full confidence in their wives?

3. How would you describe the work ethic of this woman?

DAY TWO READING AND QUESTIONS

She considers a field and buys it;
    out of her earnings she plants a vineyard.

She sets about her work vigorously;
> her arms are strong for her tasks.
She sees that her trading is profitable,
> and her lamp does not go out at night.
In her hand she holds the distaff
> and grasps the spindle with her fingers.
She opens her arms to the poor
> and extends her hands to the needy.
When it snows, she has no fear for her household;
> for all of them are clothed in scarlet. (31:16–21)

1. What does the woman do in these verses? Are these acts typically considered "women's work"?

2. What kind of businesswoman is she?

3. Why is it significant that she cares for the poor and needy? What might you think of her if she did not?

DAY THREE READING AND QUESTIONS

She makes coverings for her bed;
> she is clothed in fine linen and purple.
Her husband is respected at the city gate,
> where he takes his seat among the elders of the land.
She makes linen garments and sells them,
> and supplies the merchants with sashes.
She is clothed with strength and dignity;
> she can laugh at the days to come.
She speaks with wisdom,
> and faithful instruction is on her tongue.
She watches over the affairs of her household
> and does not eat the bread of idleness. (31:22–27)

1. How would you describe the economic status of this woman and her family? Why do they have this status?

2. How do the actions of this woman affect the life and status of her husband?

3. This woman not only acts wisely but speaks wisely. Why is this important in light of what we have studied in Proverbs?

DAY FOUR READING AND QUESTIONS

Her children arise and call her blessed;
    her husband also, and he praises her:
"Many women do noble things,
    but you surpass them all."
Charm is deceptive, and beauty is fleeting;
    but a woman who fears the LORD is to be praised.
Honor her for all that her hands have done,
    and let her works bring her praise at the city gate. (31:28–31)

1. How important is it that her children and husband praise the woman? Why do they praise her? Is it good to seek praise? How important is praise in your life?

2. What value does our culture place on charm and beauty?

3. How does this woman show that she fears the Lord?

DAY FIVE READING AND QUESTIONS

Go back and read Proverbs 31:10–31.

1. How are women pictured in Proverbs?

2. How does the description of this woman compare to that of Lady Wisdom in the previous section?

3. What does it take to be wise for a lifetime?

Meditation on A Lifetime of Wisdom (31:10–31)

What does it take to be a worthwhile person? What does it take to be a woman of worth?

Proverbs says many things about women, some negative, some positive. Here we have the ideal woman pictured.

But this "ideal" is not completely stereotypical of the traditional "good wife." Her worth is not based on the status of her husband. She is more than "Mrs. He Who Sits at the Gates." Her worth is more than being a good mother, although she provides food and clothing for her family. Unlike our current society, her worth is not based on appearance. It is not based on good manners or on following the norms of the culture. Her worth is based on her actions, her work, much of which is not traditionally thought of as woman's work.

Her worth is based on her fear of the Lord: "Charm is deceptive, and beauty is fleeting; but a woman who fears the LORD is to be praised." Her worth springs from wisdom—a lifetime of wisdom. She embodies Lady Wisdom herself.

And just as advice from father to son in Proverbs applies also to women, so men should follow the path of this wise woman. That means women and men should be less concerned with the norms of their culture and more attune to the Lord who gives wisdom.

"Giving Lord, grant us wisdom like this woman!"

MEDITATIONS

ECCLESIASTES
PASSAGES FROM THE NEW LIVING TRANSLATION

THE LIMITS OF WISDOM
1:1–18

DAY ONE READING AND QUESTIONS

These are the words of the Teacher, King David's son, who ruled in Jerusalem.

"Everything is meaningless," says the Teacher, "completely meaningless!"

What do people get for all their hard work under the sun? (1:1–3)

1. *What does a title like "the Teacher" have to do with wisdom?*

2. *Is everything meaningless? Why would the Bible say such a thing?*

3. *What answer does the writer expect from the question, "What do people get for all their hard work under the sun?"*

DAY TWO READING AND QUESTIONS

Generations come and generations go, but the earth never changes. The sun rises and the sun sets, then hurries around to rise again. The wind blows south, and then turns north. Around and around it goes, blowing in circles. Rivers run into the sea, but the sea is never full. Then the water returns again to the rivers and flows out again to the sea. Everything is wearisome beyond description. No matter how much we see, we are never satisfied. No matter how much we hear, we are not content.

History merely repeats itself. It has all been done before. Nothing under the sun is truly new. Sometimes people say, "Here is something new!" But actually it is old; nothing is ever truly new. We don't remember what happened in the past, and in future generations, no one will remember what we are doing now. (1:4–11)

1. Why does the endless cycle of nature seem wearisome?

2. If there is nothing new under the sun, how does that make you feel?

3. What is the result of not remembering what happened in the past?

DAY THREE READING AND QUESTIONS

I, the Teacher, was king of Israel, and I lived in Jerusalem. I devoted myself to search for understanding and to explore by wisdom everything being done under heaven. I soon discovered that God has dealt a tragic existence to the human race. I observed everything going on under the sun, and really, it is all meaningless—like chasing the wind.
   What is wrong cannot be made right.
   What is missing cannot be recovered. (1:12–15)

1. How has God dealt a tragic existence to the human race?

2. What does it mean to chase after the wind? What are the results of chasing after the wind?

3. If we cannot right wrongs, how does that make us feel?

DAY FOUR READING AND QUESTIONS

I said to myself, "Look, I am wiser than any of the kings who ruled in Jerusalem before me. I have greater wisdom and knowledge than any of them." So I set out to learn everything from wisdom to madness and folly. But I learned firsthand that pursuing all this is like chasing the wind.

> The greater my wisdom, the greater my grief.
> To increase knowledge only increases sorrow. (1:16–18)

1. How did the writer of Ecclesiastes get wisdom?

2. How is getting wisdom like chasing the wind?

3. Why would wisdom bring sorrow and grief?

DAY FIVE READING AND QUESTIONS

Go back and read Ecclesiastes 1:1–18.

1. How is the tone of Ecclesiastes different from that of Proverbs?

2. Is meaning to be found in new things and experiences? Why or why not?

3. Wisdom is always a blessing in Proverbs. In Ecclesiastes, wisdom brings sorrow. How can both be true?

Meditation on the Limits of Wisdom (1:1–18)

In Proverbs, traditional wisdom solves our problems. So saying, "There is nothing new under the sun," may sound like good news. There is no situation where the traditional answers do not apply.

But in Ecclesiastes, the sameness of each day is bad news. It is wearisome. Today looks just like yesterday, and tomorrow will be more of the same.

In Ecclesiastes, the traditional wisdom that promises easy answers does not always deliver. Seeking wisdom is like chasing the wind. It only brings sorrow and grief.

How can wisdom be such a blessing in Proverbs and such a curse in Ecclesiastes? Because traditional wisdom can only take us so far. It's not that our parents taught us falsehoods; it's that the truths they taught us do not always work. As we grow older, we find that the world is more complicated. We find that the black-and-white answers of our childhood soon change to shades of gray.

Ecclesiastes points us to a deeper wisdom. Or better, it points us beyond the wisdom we have learned to a trust that transcends wisdom. Fear of the Lord, trusting in God particularly when the old wisdom fails us, creates an even deeper relationship with God. We do not have the answers to life. We cannot find the answers to life. But we trust the love of God.

"God of love, give us the wisdom to know the limits of wisdom."

THE LIMITS OF WORK
2:4–26

DAY ONE READING AND QUESTIONS

I also tried to find meaning by building huge homes for myself and by planting beautiful vineyards. I made gardens and parks, filling them with all kinds of fruit trees. I built reservoirs to collect the water to irrigate my many flourishing groves. I bought slaves, both men and women, and others were born into my household. I also owned large herds and flocks, more than any of the kings who had lived in Jerusalem before me. I collected great sums of silver and gold, the treasure of many kings and provinces. I hired wonderful singers, both men and women, and had many beautiful concubines. I had everything a man could desire!

So I became greater than all who had lived in Jerusalem before me, and my wisdom never failed me. (2:4–9)

1. What projects did the writer of Ecclesiastes undertake? Are all these good projects?

2. How do these projects reflect the value of work spoken of in Proverbs?

3. Why does the writer add, "my wisdom never failed me," after listing his projects?

DAY TWO READING AND QUESTIONS

Anything I wanted, I would take. I denied myself no pleasure. I even found great pleasure in hard work, a reward for all my labors. But as I looked at everything I had worked so hard to accomplish, it was all so meaningless—like chasing the wind. There was nothing really worthwhile anywhere.

So I decided to compare wisdom with foolishness and madness (for who can do this better than I, the king?). I thought, "Wisdom is better than foolishness, just as light is better than darkness. For the wise can see where they are going, but fools walk in the dark." Yet I saw that the wise and the foolish share the same fate. Both will die. (2:10–15)

1. What does it mean to have pleasure in hard work?

2. Why were all his accomplishments meaningless?

3. Why is wisdom better than foolishness? What do the wise know that the foolish do not know?

DAY THREE READING AND QUESTIONS

So I said to myself, "Since I will end up the same as the fool, what's the value of all my wisdom? This is all so meaningless!" For the wise and the foolish both die. The wise will not be remembered any longer than the fool. In the days to come, both will be forgotten.

So I came to hate life because everything done here under the sun is so troubling. Everything is meaningless—like chasing the wind.

I came to hate all my hard work here on earth, for I must leave to others everything I have earned. And who can tell whether my successors will be wise or foolish? Yet they will control everything I have gained by my skill and hard work under the sun. How meaningless! So I gave up in despair, questioning the value of all my hard work in this world. (2:15–20)

1. How does death limit the worth of work?

2. What will happen to all our accomplishments when we die?

3. Why is work meaningless?

DAY FOUR READING AND QUESTIONS

Some people work wisely with knowledge and skill, then must leave the fruit of their efforts to someone who hasn't worked for it. This, too, is meaningless, a great tragedy. So what do people get in this life for all their hard work and anxiety? Their days of labor are filled with pain and grief; even at night their minds cannot rest. It is all meaningless.

So I decided there is nothing better than to enjoy food and drink and to find satisfaction in work. Then I realized that these pleasures are from the hand of God. For who can eat or enjoy anything apart from him? God gives wisdom, knowledge, and joy to those who please him. But if a sinner becomes wealthy, God takes the wealth away and gives it to those who please him. This, too, is meaningless—like chasing the wind. (2:21–26)

1. What comes to mind when you think of hard work?

2. When does work become anxious striving?

3. How can one find satisfaction in work?

DAY FIVE READING AND QUESTIONS

Go back and read Ecclesiastes 2:4–26.

1. Is work a good thing or a bad thing in these verses?

2. When does work become hard labor?

3. Who can bring us happiness in our work?

Meditation on the Limits of Work (2:4–26)

In Proverbs, work is a blessing. If one works hard, prosperity and wisdom follow.

Ecclesiastes reminds us that work can be a burden. Work becomes toil—repetitive, back-breaking, endless work. And yet Ecclesiastes also says we can find happiness and joy in our work. How can both be true?

The key here is the reason for our work. If we work to provide for ourselves, our families, and those in need, then we can find meaning in the work, no matter how hard and boring it may be. However, work becomes toil if we think it will lead to lasting results.

This is the opposite of our society's view of work. Our society values work that accomplishes great things. Work that will be remembered after we are gone. But Ecclesiastes tells us that our great accomplishments will not be remembered, and that at death we must leave our legacies to those who might undo all the good we think we have done. Thus, working to accomplish great things is meaningless.

Who has the best job, the president of a company or the night janitor? The answer is clear in our culture. The president is the boss. The president makes more money, has more influence, and accomplishes great things. The president is praised and honored. The janitor has a low-paying, menial, unnoticed job. The janitor accomplishes nothing that lasts. What is cleaned today must be cleaned again tomorrow.

But what if the janitor does his job with joy? What if he does it to provide for those around him? What if he does it for the Lord? And what if the president spends most of her time in anxious striving over what is beyond her control? Who has happiness in their work? Who has toil?

"God of work and rest, grant us happiness in our work. Keep us from anxious striving."

THE LIMITS OF TIMING
3:1–4:6

DAY ONE READING AND QUESTIONS

For everything there is a season,
    a time for every activity under heaven.
A time to be born and a time to die.
    A time to plant and a time to harvest.
A time to kill and a time to heal.
    A time to tear down and a time to build up.
A time to cry and a time to laugh.
    A time to grieve and a time to dance.
A time to scatter stones and a time to gather stones.
    A time to embrace and a time to turn away.
A time to search and a time to quit searching.
    A time to keep and a time to throw away.
A time to tear and a time to mend.
    A time to be quiet and a time to speak.
A time to love and a time to hate.
    A time for war and a time for peace. (3:1–8)

1. *How important is timing in life?*

2. *When would be the time for the destructive items in this list—killing, uprooting, tearing, hating, and warring? Should we not avoid these things at all times?*

3. *Which items on this list reflect the sayings in the book of Proverbs?*

DAY TWO READING AND QUESTIONS

What do people really get for all their hard work? I have seen the burden God has placed on us all. Yet God has made everything beautiful for its own time. He has planted eternity in the human heart, but even so, people cannot see the whole scope of God's work from beginning to end. So I concluded there is nothing better than to be happy and enjoy ourselves as long as we can. And people should eat and drink and enjoy the fruits of their labor, for these are gifts from God.

And I know that whatever God does is final. Nothing can be added to it or taken from it. God's purpose is that people should fear him. What is happening now has happened before, and what will happen in the future has happened before, because God makes the same things happen over and over again.

I also noticed that under the sun there is evil in the courtroom. Yes, even the courts of law are corrupt! I said to myself, "In due season God will judge everyone, both good and bad, for all their deeds." (3:9–17)

1. Since "people cannot see the whole scope of God's work from beginning to end," can humans usually tell the right time for certain actions?

2. What does wrong timing have to do with injustice?

3. When will be the time for God's judgment?

DAY THREE READING AND QUESTIONS

I also thought about the human condition—how God proves to people that they are like animals. For people and animals share the same fate—both breathe and both must die. So people have no real advantage over the animals. How meaningless! Both go to the same place—they came from dust and they return to dust. For who can prove that the human spirit goes up and the spirit of animals goes down into the earth? So I saw that there is nothing better for people than to be happy in their work. That is our lot in life. And no one can bring us back to see what happens after we die. (3:18–22)

1. Does the writer of Ecclesiastes believe in life after death?

2. If not, why should one fear God if there is no afterlife?

3. If we cannot see what happens after us, how can we know the right timing in life? How do we know which of our actions will have lasting value?

DAY FOUR READING AND QUESTIONS

Again, I observed all the oppression that takes place under the sun. I saw the tears of the oppressed, with no one to comfort them. The oppressors have great power, and their victims are helpless. So I concluded that the dead are better off than the living. But most fortunate of all are those who are not yet born. For they have not seen all the evil that is done under the sun.

Then I observed that most people are motivated to success because they envy their neighbors. But this, too, is meaningless— like chasing the wind.

"Fools fold their idle hands,
   leading them to ruin."

And yet,

"Better to have one handful with quietness
   than two handfuls with hard work
   and chasing the wind." (4:1–6)

1. Is there truly no comforter for the oppressed? According to Proverbs, who is the comforter?

2. How does achievement spring from envy?

3. What does success have to do with injustice?

DAY FIVE READING AND QUESTIONS

Go back and read Ecclesiastes 3:1–4:6.

1. Can humans really know the right time for their actions? Who alone knows the right time?

2. What is the connection between the finality of death and injustice?

3. Do these verses seem uniformly depressing, or is there any good news in this passage?

Meditation on the Limits of Timing (3:1–4:6)

My musical tastes are stuck in the 1960s and '70s, so I remember some of these verses from Ecclesiastes because they make up most of the lyrics of "Turn, Turn, Turn," written by Pete Seeger and made famous by the Byrds. Seeger turns the words into an antiwar song by adding, "I swear it's not too late," after the verse about "a time for peace."

Many hear that song and see these verses as a call to discern what time it is. If only we could get the timing of our lives right, all would be fine.

However, if you keep reading in this passage, you find that we cannot get the timing right. "I have seen the burden God has laid on the human race. He has made everything beautiful in its time. He has also set eternity in the human heart; yet no one can fathom what God has done from beginning to end." We want to see the big picture ("eternity") and get the timing right, but God alone knows the right time. We blunder along as best we can, often with bad timing.

So the song we should sing is "Does Anybody Really Know What Time It Is?" (written by Robert Lamm of Chicago). Ecclesiastes reminds us that we do not even know the time of our death or what happens after we die.

Since that is true, injustice seems to reign. Those oppressed in this life seem to be without hope.

But as Christians, we have a better hope. We believe in resurrection because Christ has been raised from the dead. We believe the whole creation will be transformed into a new heaven and earth where justice will rule. God will defend the oppressed and make things right.

But we do not see it yet. And we do not have all the answers. We need the humility to admit that we walk by faith, not by sight. We do not know the right time for many things in our lives. But we trust the one who holds eternity.

"God who knows all, may we trust your timing, even when we do not understand what time it is."

THE LIMITS OF WEALTH
5:8–6:9

DAY ONE READING AND QUESTIONS

Don't be surprised if you see a poor person being oppressed by the powerful and if justice is being miscarried throughout the land. For every official is under orders from higher up, and matters of justice get lost in red tape and bureaucracy. Even the king milks the land for his own profit!

Those who love money will never have enough. How meaningless to think that wealth brings true happiness! The more you have, the more people come to help you spend it. So what good is wealth—except perhaps to watch it slip through your fingers!

People who work hard sleep well, whether they eat little or much. But the rich seldom get a good night's sleep. (5:8–12)

1. According to these verses, why is there injustice in the land?

2. What are the harmful effects of riches in these verses?

3. Why would abundance of riches lead to lack of sleep?

DAY TWO READING AND QUESTIONS

There is another serious problem I have seen under the sun. Hoarding riches harms the saver. Money is put into risky investments that turn sour, and everything is lost. In the end, there is nothing left to pass on to one's children. We all come to the end of our lives as naked and empty-handed as on the day we were born. We can't take our riches with us.

And this, too, is a very serious problem. People leave this world no better off than when they came. All their hard work is for nothing—like working for the wind. Throughout their lives, they live under a cloud—frustrated, discouraged, and angry. (5:13–16)

1. What does it mean to hoard wealth? Why would one hoard? How can one keep from hoarding?

2. "You can't take it with you" is a good summary of this passage. How does knowing this change the way we treat money?

3. How does wealth lead to great frustration, discouragement, and anger?

DAY THREE READING AND QUESTIONS

Even so, I have noticed one thing, at least, that is good. It is good for people to eat, drink, and enjoy their work under the sun during the short life God has given them, and to accept their lot in life. And it is a good thing to receive wealth from God and the good health to enjoy it. To enjoy your work and accept your lot in life—this is indeed a gift from God. God keeps such people so busy enjoying life that they take no time to brood over the past.

There is another serious tragedy I have seen under the sun, and it weighs heavily on humanity. God gives some people great wealth and honor and everything they could ever want, but then he doesn't give them the chance to enjoy these things. They die, and someone else, even a stranger, ends up enjoying their wealth! This is meaningless—a sickening tragedy. (5:18–6:2)

1. Who gives the ability to enjoy wealth? How does this change how one views wealth?

2. *Is it good not to reflect on the days of your life? Shouldn't we be reflective?*

3. *How can one have wealth, possessions, and honor and not enjoy them? What does it mean to be content?*

DAY FOUR READING AND QUESTIONS

A man might have a hundred children and live to be very old. But if he finds no satisfaction in life and doesn't even get a decent burial, it would have been better for him to be born dead. His birth would have been meaningless, and he would have ended in darkness. He wouldn't even have had a name, and he would never have seen the sun or known of its existence. Yet he would have had more peace than in growing up to be an unhappy man. He might live a thousand years twice over but still not find contentment. And since he must die like everyone else—well, what's the use?

All people spend their lives scratching for food, but they never seem to have enough. So are wise people really better off than fools? Do poor people gain anything by being wise and knowing how to act in front of others?

Enjoy what you have rather than desiring what you don't have. Just dreaming about nice things is meaningless—like chasing the wind. (6:3–9)

1. *How much money should satisfy us? If we are not satisfied, what are we left with?*

2. *Is poverty with wisdom better than riches?*

3. *How is dreaming about nice things like chasing the wind?*

DAY FIVE READING AND QUESTIONS

Go back and read Ecclesiastes 5:8–6:9.

1. Do you make more money now than you did ten years ago? If so, are you happier?

2. If you had more money, would you worry less or more?

3. How much money does your family really need?

Meditation on the Limits of Wealth (5:8–6:9)

I have a secret, a guaranteed way for you to make all the money you would ever want. Here it is:

Be content with what you have now.

Easier said than done. If only we had a bit more money, we'd have less worry and more security. We'd be able to enjoy life more. We could provide for our family better.

The most powerful idol in our world is the great god called "The Economy." This god is spoken of on every television show, seen on every billboard, and even finds its way into the church. We measure people by their net worth. We look at the bottom line. We want to get ahead. All these well-known phrases show that our real god is money. It's money that matters. The god economy whispers that most obscene four-letter word in our ears: "more, more, more."

But Ecclesiastes says the exact opposite. More money leads to more worry. If you don't enjoy the money you have now, you won't enjoy more money. You don't know what will happen in the future, so you can't guarantee provision for your family.

So how do we handle money? First, we remember it is a gift of God. No matter how hard we work for it, God alone provides daily bread. And no matter how much or how little we make, God alone gives the gift of enjoyment.

You can't take it with you. Money won't buy you happiness.

We can have God with us. He can make us happy.

"God of love, take the love of money from our hearts. Give us enjoyment in what we have."

WISDOM LIMITED BY AGE
11:7–12:8

DAY ONE READING AND QUESTIONS

Light is sweet; how pleasant to see a new day dawning.
When people live to be very old, let them rejoice in every day of life. But let them also remember there will be many dark days. Everything still to come is meaningless.
Young people, it's wonderful to be young! Enjoy every minute of it. Do everything you want to do; take it all in. But remember that you must give an account to God for everything you do. So refuse to worry, and keep your body healthy. But remember that youth, with a whole life before you, is meaningless. (11:7–10)

1. How can one enjoy life if everything is meaningless?

2. How will God judge the young regarding what they enjoy?

3. Why are youth and vigor meaningless?

DAY TWO READING AND QUESTIONS

Don't let the excitement of youth cause you to forget your Creator. Honor him in your youth before you grow old and say, "Life is not pleasant anymore." Remember him before the light of the sun, moon, and stars is dim to your old eyes, and rain clouds continually darken your sky. (12:1–2)

1. What does it mean to remember and honor our Creator?

2. Is there no pleasure in being old?

3. Why does the world grow dim when we grow old? Is this more than losing our eyesight?

DAY THREE READING AND QUESTIONS

Remember him before your legs—the guards of your house—start to tremble; and before your shoulders—the strong men—stoop. Remember him before your teeth—your few remaining servants—stop grinding; and before your eyes—the women looking through the windows—see dimly.

Remember him before the door to life's opportunities is closed and the sound of work fades. Now you rise at the first chirping of the birds, but then all their sounds will grow faint. (12:3–4)

1. Old people usually lose the ability to walk. What are the results of this loss?

2. How does loss of teeth affect old people?

3. Loss of hearing is also part of these verses. Why is this such a great loss?

DAY FOUR READING AND QUESTIONS

Remember him before you become fearful of falling and worry about danger in the streets; before your hair turns white like an almond tree in bloom, and you drag along without energy like a dying grasshopper, and the caperberry no longer inspires sexual desire. Remember him before you near the grave, your everlasting home, when the mourners will weep at your funeral.

Yes, remember your Creator now while you are young, before the silver cord of life snaps and the golden bowl is broken. Don't wait until the water jar is smashed at the spring and the pulley is broken at the well. For then the dust will return to the earth, and the spirit will return to God who gave it.

"Everything is meaningless," says the Teacher, "completely meaningless." (12:5–8)

1. *Old people often live in fear. Why do you think that is?*

2. *What are the pictures of death in these verses?*

3. *How does death make everything meaningless?*

DAY FIVE READING AND QUESTIONS

Go back and read Ecclesiastes 11:7–12:8.

1. *What advantages are there to being young?*

2. *What advantages are there to being old?*

3. *Is it easier to serve God when young or when old? Why?*

Meditation on Wisdom Limited by Age (11:7–12:8)

"After age sixty, it's nothing but patch, patch, patch."

So said my mother-in-law about her own health.

Ecclesiastes agrees. The evil days come. Eyesight fails. Hearing goes. One walks cautiously, afraid of the fall that leads to the hospital. Old age is tough.

Proverbs praises old age because with it often comes wisdom. In Proverbs, youth is tied to folly.

But Ecclesiastes turns that around. "Don't let the excitement of youth cause you to forget your Creator. Honor him in your youth before you grow old and say, 'Life is not pleasant anymore.'" In Proverbs, youthful pleasures are a snare, often leading to foolish acts. But Ecclesiastes says the young should enjoy their pleasures while they are young, as long as they remember that the Creator is the source of those pleasures.

On the other hand, old age is, at best, a mixed blessing. One may obtain wisdom, but one slowly loses the pleasure of health.

So who has it best, the young or the old? Ecclesiastes reminds us that all should remember their Creator. The young in their youthful folly and the old in their declining health. Every age is the right age to fear God.

"God of all ages, give us the joy of youth and the wisdom of age."

MEDITATIONS

JOB
PASSAGES FROM THE ENGLISH STANDARD VERSION

THE LORD NOTICES JOB
1:1–22

DAY ONE READING AND QUESTIONS

There was a man in the land of Uz whose name was Job, and that man was blameless and upright, one who feared God and turned away from evil. There were born to him seven sons and three daughters. He possessed 7,000 sheep, 3,000 camels, 500 yoke of oxen, and 500 female donkeys, and very many servants, so that this man was the greatest of all the people of the east. His sons used to go and hold a feast in the house of each one on his day, and they would send and invite their three sisters to eat and drink with them. And when the days of the feast had run their course, Job would send and consecrate them, and he would rise early in the morning and offer burnt offerings according to the number of them all. For Job said, "It may be that my children have sinned, and cursed God in their hearts." Thus Job did continually. (1:1–5)

1. How is Job described in these verses?

2. Uz is in the east. This means Job is not from Israel. Why is that significant?

3. Why do you think Job consecrates and sacrifices for his children?

DAY TWO READING AND QUESTIONS

Now there was a day when the sons of God came to present themselves before the LORD, and Satan also came among them. The LORD said to Satan, "From where have you come?" Satan answered the Lord and said, "From going to and fro on the earth, and from walking up and down on it." And the Lord said to Satan, "Have you considered my servant Job, that there is none like him on the earth, a blameless and upright man, who fears God and turns away from evil?" Then Satan answered the Lord and said, "Does Job fear God for no reason? Have you not put a hedge around him and his house and all that he has, on every side? You have blessed the work of his hands, and his possessions have increased in the land. But stretch out your hand and touch all that he has, and he will curse you to your face." And the Lord said to Satan, "Behold, all that he has is in your hand. Only against him do not stretch out your hand." So Satan went out from the presence of the Lord. (1:6–12)

1. Why is Satan among the sons of God who appear before the Lord?

2. Why does God point out Job to Satan?

3. According to Satan, why does Job fear God?

DAY THREE READING AND QUESTIONS

Now there was a day when his sons and daughters were eating and drinking wine in their oldest brother's house, and there came a messenger to Job and said, "The oxen were plowing and the donkeys feeding beside them, and the Sabeans fell upon them and took them and struck down the servants with the edge of the sword, and I alone have escaped to tell you." While he was yet speaking, there came another and said, "The fire of God fell from heaven and burned up the sheep and the servants and consumed them, and I alone have escaped to tell you." While he was yet speaking, there came another and said, "The Chaldeans formed three groups and made a raid on the camels and took them and struck down the servants with the edge of the sword, and I alone have escaped to tell you." While he was yet speaking, there came another and said, "Your sons and daughters were eating and drinking wine in their oldest brother's house, and behold, a great wind came across the wilderness and struck the four corners of the house, and it fell upon the young people, and they are dead, and I alone have escaped to tell you." (1:13–19)

1. Why is it harder to accept bad news when it comes in bunches all at once?

2. What is harder to accept, evil from raiding armies or natural disasters like lightning and wind? Why?

3. What good did it do for Job to offer sacrifices for his children?

DAY FOUR READING AND QUESTIONS

Then Job arose and tore his robe and shaved his head and fell on the ground and worshiped. And he said, "Naked I came from my mother's womb, and naked shall I return. The LORD gave, and the LORD has taken away; blessed be the name of the LORD."
In all this Job did not sin or charge God with wrong. (1:20–22)

1. What is the meaning of Job tearing his robe and shaving his head?

2. Why does Job worship and bless God in these circumstances?

3. Why doesn't Job blame God for his terrible misfortunes?

DAY FIVE READING AND QUESTIONS

Go back and read Job 1:1–22.

1. Is God to blame for what happened to Job?

2. Why does God allow these catastrophes to happen to Job?

3. Does Job fear God for no reason?

Meditation on Job 1:1–22

Don't we want God to notice us? In the Bible, at times the Lord sees the sins and idolatry of his people and punishes them. But it is usually a good thing when the Lord remembers his people. When he sees them, he delivers and blesses them.

Not so in the book of Job.

The Lord certainly notices Job. And he notices for all the right reasons. "And the Lord said to Satan, 'Have you considered my servant Job, that there is none like him on the earth, a blameless and upright man, who fears God and turns away from evil?'" God brags on Job.

Satan has noticed Job, too. Satan cannot deny that Job is blameless, but he has an explanation for it: "Does Job fear God for no reason?" Satan says Job is good because God has protected and blessed him. Take that protection away, and Job will curse God.

So God allows Satan to harm Job. For no reason. It's almost as if the Lord and Satan have a bet over Job—which makes Job a pawn, a test case, a guinea pig.

"What kind of God does this?" That is one of the questions raised in the book of Job. Another question is the one Satan asks: "Why does Job serve the Lord?"

We still ask these questions. Who is our God? And how do we continue to follow this God when we do not like or understand his ways?

"All-powerful God, your ways are beyond us. May we serve you even when the rewards and protection do not come."

JOB TOLD TO CURSE GOD
2:1–3:26

DAY ONE READING AND QUESTIONS

Again there was a day when the sons of God came to present themselves before the Lord, and Satan also came among them to present himself before the Lord. And the Lord said to Satan, "From where have you come?" Satan answered the Lord and said, "From going to and fro on the earth, and from walking up and down on it." And the Lord said to Satan, "Have you considered my servant Job, that there is none like him on the earth, a blameless and upright man, who fears God and turns away from evil? He still holds fast his integrity, although you incited me against him to destroy him without reason." Then Satan answered the Lord and said, "Skin for skin! All that a man has he will give for his life. But stretch out your hand and touch his bone and his flesh, and he will curse you to your face." And the Lord said to Satan, "Behold, he is in your hand; only spare his life."

So Satan went out from the presence of the Lord and struck Job with loathsome sores from the sole of his foot to the crown of his head. And he took a piece of broken pottery with which to scrape himself while he sat in the ashes. (2:1–8)

1. *What does it mean for Job to hold fast his integrity? What is integrity?*

2. *What reason does the Lord give for destroying Job?*

3. *What will most people do to preserve their own skin?*

DAY TWO READING AND QUESTIONS

Then his wife said to him, "Do you still hold fast your integrity? Curse God and die." But he said to her, "You speak as one of the foolish women would speak. Shall we receive good from God, and shall we not receive evil?" In all this Job did not sin with his lips.

Now when Job's three friends heard of all this evil that had come upon him, they came each from his own place, Eliphaz the Temanite, Bildad the Shuhite, and Zophar the Naamathite. They made an appointment together to come to show him sympathy and comfort him. And when they saw him from a distance, they did not recognize him. And they raised their voices and wept, and they tore their robes and sprinkled dust on their heads toward heaven. And they sat with him on the ground seven days and seven nights, and no one spoke a word to him, for they saw that his suffering was very great. (2:9–13)

1. Why does Job's wife urge him to curse God?

2. How did Job's friends comfort him?

3. How can one comfort without words?

DAY THREE READING AND QUESTIONS

After this Job opened his mouth and cursed the day of his birth. And Job said:
"Let the day perish on which I was born,
    and the night that said,
    'A man is conceived.'
Let that day be darkness!
    May God above not seek it,
nor light shine upon it.

Let gloom and deep darkness claim it.
> Let clouds dwell upon it;
> let the blackness of the day terrify it.

That night—let thick darkness seize it!
> Let it not rejoice among the days of the year;
> let it not come into the number of the months.

Behold, let that night be barren;
> let no joyful cry enter it.

Let those curse it who curse the day,
> who are ready to rouse up Leviathan.

Let the stars of its dawn be dark;
> let it hope for light, but have none,
> nor see the eyelids of the morning,

because it did not shut the doors of my mother's womb,
> nor hide trouble from my eyes.

Why did I not die at birth,
> come out from the womb and expire?

Why did the knees receive me?
> Or why the breasts, that I should nurse?

For then I would have lain down and been quiet;
> I would have slept; then I would have been at rest,

with kings and counselors of the earth
> who rebuilt ruins for themselves,

or with princes who had gold,
> who filled their houses with silver." (3:1–15)

1. *Is Job right to curse the day he was born?*

2. *Does Job blame God for his troubles in these verses?*

3. *Why does death seem preferable to life for Job?*

DAY FOUR READING AND QUESTIONS

"Or why was I not as a hidden stillborn child,
    as infants who never see the light?
There the wicked cease from troubling,
    and there the weary are at rest.
There the prisoners are at ease together;
    they hear not the voice of the taskmaster.
The small and the great are there,
    and the slave is free from his master.
Why is light given to him who is in misery,
    and life to the bitter in soul,
who long for death, but it comes not,
    and dig for it more than for hidden treasures,
who rejoice exceedingly
    and are glad when they find the grave?
Why is light given to a man whose way is hidden,
    whom God has hedged in?
For my sighing comes instead of my bread,
    and my groanings are poured out like water.
For the thing that I fear comes upon me,
    and what I dread befalls me.
I am not at ease, nor am I quiet;
    I have no rest, but trouble comes." (3:16–26)

1. How is everyone alike in death?

2. Is light a good or a bad thing in these verses? Why?

3. In Job 1:10, Satan says God had placed a hedge of protection around Job. In these verses, what does the hedge do?

DAY FIVE READING AND QUESTIONS

Go back and read Job 2:1–3:26.

1. Why does God allow Satan to attack Job's body?

2. Why doesn't Job curse God and die, as his wife suggests?

3. What are some things that are worse than death?

Meditation on Job 2:1–3:26

"Curse God and die." Why would Job's wife say this? Is she just an evil woman? That's hard to believe, considering how righteous Job is. So why say such a thing?

Because she knows Job. Most wives know their husbands better than anyone. She knows Job is not sinless, but she also knows he has not done anything recently that would cause God to take away Job's wealth, family, and health. If Job is innocent, then God must be guilty. The Lord must be an evil God, so curse him!

Job thinks otherwise. Yes, Job knows he has done nothing to deserve this from God. But he also knows he did not fully deserve blessings from God. "Shall we receive good from God, and shall we not receive evil?" He calls his wife foolish. Not because she does not understand Job (she does). Not because she doesn't understand God (she doesn't, and neither does Job). But because she will not accept a God she does not like or understand.

This is not to minimize her pain or Job's pain. Job wishes he were dead. But he will not charge the Lord with wrongdoing.

How about us? When trouble comes, do we blame ourselves, even when we are not to blame? Do we blame God? Do we defend God? Or are we willing, like Job (and at this point his friends), to pour out our complaint or to sit in silence not knowing why God has allowed this?

"O Lord, your ways are not our ways! May we accept what you give and what you take away."

JOB'S FRIENDS BLAME JOB
4:1–21; 6:1–30

DAY ONE READING AND QUESTIONS

Then Eliphaz the Temanite answered and said:
  "If one ventures a word with you, will you be impatient?
    Yet who can keep from speaking?
  Behold, you have instructed many,
    and you have strengthened the weak hands.
  Your words have upheld him who was stumbling,
    and you have made firm the feeble knees.
  But now it has come to you, and you are impatient;
    it touches you, and you are dismayed.
  Is not your fear of God your confidence,
    and the integrity of your ways your hope?
  Remember: who that was innocent ever perished?
    Or where were the upright cut off?
  As I have seen, those who plow iniquity
    and sow trouble reap the same.
  By the breath of God they perish,
    and by the blast of his anger they are consumed.
  The roar of the lion, the voice of the fierce lion,
    the teeth of the young lions are broken.
  The strong lion perishes for lack of prey,
    and the cubs of the lioness are scattered." (4:1–11)

1. *Eliphaz says Job corrected others but cannot take correction. Why is it easier to give than to take correction?*

2. In your experience, have the innocent ever perished? Why is Eliphaz so sure this never happens?

3. Do we always reap what we sow?

DAY TWO READING AND QUESTIONS

"Now a word was brought to me stealthily;
    my ear received the whisper of it.
Amid thoughts from visions of the night,
    when deep sleep falls on men,
dread came upon me, and trembling,
    which made all my bones shake.
A spirit glided past my face;
    the hair of my flesh stood up.
It stood still,
    but I could not discern its appearance.
A form was before my eyes;
    there was silence, then I heard a voice:
'Can mortal man be in the right before God?
    Can a man be pure before his Maker?
Even in his servants he puts no trust,
    and his angels he charges with error;
how much more those who dwell in houses of clay,
    whose foundation is in the dust,
    who are crushed like the moth.
Between morning and evening they are beaten to pieces;
    they perish forever without anyone regarding it.
Is not their tent-cord plucked up within them,
    do they not die, and that without wisdom?'" (4:12–21)

1. Can humans be right and pure before God?

2. *Eliphaz is obviously accusing Job of sin. Did Job sin?*

3. *According to Eliphaz, does Job deserve what has happened to him?*

DAY THREE READING AND QUESTIONS

Then Job answered and said:
  "Oh that my vexation were weighed,
    and all my calamity laid in the balances!
For then it would be heavier than the sand of the sea;
  therefore my words have been rash.
For the arrows of the Almighty are in me;
  my spirit drinks their poison;
  the terrors of God are arrayed against me.
Does the wild donkey bray when he has grass,
  or the ox low over his fodder?
Can that which is tasteless be eaten without salt,
  or is there any taste in the juice of the mallow?
My appetite refuses to touch them;
  they are as food that is loathsome to me.
Oh that I might have my request,
  and that God would fulfill my hope,
that it would please God to crush me,
  that he would let loose his hand and cut me off!
This would be my comfort;
  I would even exult in pain unsparing,
  for I have not denied the words of the Holy One.
What is my strength, that I should wait?
  And what is my end, that I should be patient?
Is my strength the strength of stones, or is my flesh bronze?
Have I any help in me,
  when resource is driven from me?" (6:1–13)

1. Whom does Job blame for his troubles? Is he right to place the blame there?

2. What does Job want God to do to him?

3. What does Job mean when he says, "I have not denied the words of the Holy One"?

DAY FOUR READING AND QUESTIONS

"He who withholds kindness from a friend
    forsakes the fear of the Almighty.
My brothers are treacherous as a torrent-bed,
    as torrential streams that pass away,
which are dark with ice,
    and where the snow hides itself.
When they melt, they disappear;
    when it is hot, they vanish from their place.
The caravans turn aside from their course;
    they go up into the waste and perish.
The caravans of Tema look,
    the travelers of Sheba hope.
They are ashamed because they were confident;
    they come there and are disappointed.
For you have now become nothing;
    you see my calamity and are afraid.
Have I said, 'Make me a gift'?
    Or, 'From your wealth offer a bribe for me'?
Or, 'Deliver me from the adversary's hand'?
    Or, 'Redeem me from the hand of the ruthless'?
Teach me, and I will be silent;
    make me understand how I have gone astray.

> How forceful are upright words!
>> But what does reproof from you reprove?
> Do you think that you can reprove words,
>> when the speech of a despairing man is wind?
> You would even cast lots over the fatherless,
>> and bargain over your friend.
> But now, be pleased to look at me,
>> for I will not lie to your face.
> Please turn; let no injustice be done.
>> Turn now; my vindication is at stake.
> Is there any injustice on my tongue?
>> Cannot my palate discern the cause of calamity?" (6:14–30)

1. How does Job describe his friends?

2. Job says his friends are afraid of his calamity. Why are they afraid?

3. Why does Job think he will be vindicated?

DAY FIVE READING AND QUESTIONS

Go back and read Job 4:1–21; 6:1–30.

1. Why is Eliphaz (and the rest of Job's friends) so sure that Job deserves his troubles?

2. Here (and later in the book) Job clearly blames God for his troubles. Is Job right to do so?

3. Were Job's friends better comforters before they began to speak? Why or why not?

Meditation on Job 4:1–21; 6:1–30

Job's wife has it figured out. Job is innocent. God sent all this calamity on Job. God must be evil. "Curse God and die."

Job's friends have it figured out. God is just. He sent all this calamity on Job. So Job must be evil. So Job should confess, repent, and turn to God.

Job does not have it figured out. He knows he is innocent. He does not understand why God did this to him. But Job is not willing to break relationship with the God he does not understand.

The bulk of the book of Job is a series of speeches from Job's friends and a series of replies from Job. As the book goes on, the language of the friends becomes stronger. Job is a terrible sinner, perhaps the worst ever. The friends think they are defending the Lord.

Job's language also becomes stronger as the book goes on. He is completely bewildered by the actions of God and the words of his friends. But still, the Lord is his God. Job waits for the Lord when it makes no sense to wait.

When trouble comes to us, we want an explanation, just as Job wanted an explanation. There are plenty of folks who will use lots of words to explain. They blame God. "I can't believe in a God who would allow that." But we don't get to choose our God. There is only One. Or, if they are good church folk, they blame us. "You must have done something to deserve this."

Job does not accept those explanations. Neither should we.

"Sovereign Lord, do not lead us to the time of trial."

JOB MAINTAINS HIS INNOCENCE
31:1–40

DAY ONE READING AND QUESTIONS

"I have made a covenant with my eyes;
    how then could I gaze at a virgin?
What would be my portion from God above
    and my heritage from the Almighty on high?
Is not calamity for the unrighteous,
    and disaster for the workers of iniquity?
Does not he see my ways
    and number all my steps?
If I have walked with falsehood
    and my foot has hastened to deceit;
(Let me be weighed in a just balance,
    and let God know my integrity!)
if my step has turned aside from the way
    and my heart has gone after my eyes,
    and if any spot has stuck to my hands,
then let me sow, and another eat,
    and let what grows for me be rooted out.
If my heart has been enticed toward a woman,
    and I have lain in wait at my neighbor's door,
then let my wife grind for another,
    and let others bow down on her.
For that would be a heinous crime;
    that would be an iniquity to be punished by the judges;
for that would be a fire that consumes as far as Abaddon,
    and it would burn to the root all my increase." (31:1–12)

1. Why is it important that God sees all that Job does? Is Job trying to deceive God and others?

2. Why is it important for Job to not even gaze at a virgin?

3. How does Job's faithfulness to his wife relate to his faithfulness to God?

DAY TWO READING AND QUESTIONS

"If I have rejected the cause of my manservant or
   my maidservant,
      when they brought a complaint against me,
what then shall I do when God rises up?
   When he makes inquiry, what shall I answer him?
Did not he who made me in the womb make him?
   And did not one fashion us in the womb?
If I have withheld anything that the poor desired,
   or have caused the eyes of the widow to fail,
or have eaten my morsel alone,
   and the fatherless has not eaten of it
(for from my youth the fatherless grew up with me as with
   a father,
   and from my mother's womb I guided the widow),
if I have seen anyone perish for lack of clothing,
   or the needy without covering,
if his body has not blessed me,
   and if he was not warmed with the fleece of my sheep,
if I have raised my hand against the fatherless,
   because I saw my help in the gate,
then let my shoulder blade fall from my shoulder,
   and let my arm be broken from its socket.
For I was in terror of calamity from God,
   and I could not have faced his majesty." (31:13–23)

1. Why does Job think he should be fair to his servants?

2. What other groups of people did Job care for? Why?

3. What part did fear have in Job's care for others?

DAY THREE READING AND QUESTIONS

"If I have made gold my trust
    or called fine gold my confidence,
if I have rejoiced because my wealth was abundant
    or because my hand had found much,
if I have looked at the sun when it shone,
    or the moon moving in splendor,
and my heart has been secretly enticed,
    and my mouth has kissed my hand,
this also would be an iniquity to be punished by the judges,
    for I would have been false to God above. (31:24–28)

1. Job is very rich. What is his attitude toward wealth?

2. Why would Job not look at the sun or moon?

3. Sun, moon, and money can all be idols. What does Job think should happen to those who worship idols?

DAY FOUR READING AND QUESTIONS

"If I have rejoiced at the ruin of him who hated me,
    or exulted when evil overtook him

>   (I have not let my mouth sin
>   by asking for his life with a curse),
>   if the men of my tent have not said,
>   'Who is there that has not been filled with his meat?'
>   (the sojourner has not lodged in the street;
>   I have opened my doors to the traveler),
>   if I have concealed my transgressions as others do
>   by hiding my iniquity in my heart,
>   because I stood in great fear of the multitude,
>   and the contempt of families terrified me,
>   so that I kept silence, and did not go out of doors—
>   Oh, that I had one to hear me!
>   (Here is my signature! Let the Almighty answer me!)
>   Oh, that I had the indictment written by my adversary!
>   Surely I would carry it on my shoulder;
>   I would bind it on me as a crown;
>   I would give him an account of all my steps;
>   like a prince I would approach him.
>   If my land has cried out against me
>   and its furrows have wept together,
>   if I have eaten its yield without payment
>   and made its owners breathe their last,
>   let thorns grow instead of wheat,
>   and foul weeds instead of barley." (31:29–40)

1. *How has Job treated his enemies?*

2. *Job wants his day in court with God. What does he expect the Almighty to say to him?*

3. *How has Job treated his land? Why is that important?*

DAY FIVE READING AND QUESTIONS

Go back and read Job 31:1–40.

1. In these verses, which of the Ten Commandments has Job kept?

2. Why does Job insist on his innocence? Is this honesty or pride or self-deception?

3. Who does Job expect to vindicate him?

Meditation on Job 31:1–40

The People's Court. Judge Judy. Judge Mathis. These and other courtroom shows have been popular on television. Why? Perhaps we are interested in the messy lives of others. But part of their appeal is our deeply rooted desire for justice. When people are treated unfairly, we want to see things put right. We especially want it if we are the ones who are innocent.

So it is with Job. God had taken his wealth, his family, his health, and his reputation. For no reason. This was not punishment from God (as his friends insisted over and over again), for Job does not deserve punishment. He is innocent!

How innocent is he? It seems Job was not a Jew. He likely lived before Moses; yet he keeps the Law before the Law is given. He does not covet his neighbor's wife. He cares for the poor and oppressed. He does not trust in riches. He even cares for the land he has been given. Job's actions even reflect some of the later teachings of Jesus. He does not even look at a woman to lust after her. He does not take revenge on his enemies.

Yet Job suffers. How can he get justice? What court can he go to?

Job asks for God to judge him. He begs for answers, for vindication. "Oh, that I had one to hear me!" he cries.

And God will answer. But not the way Job expects.

"God of justice, may we trust in your vindication, even when we do not yet experience it."

THE LORD ANSWERS JOB
38:1–11; 40:1–5; 42:1–17

DAY ONE READING AND QUESTIONS

Then the LORD answered Job out of the whirlwind and said:
"Who is this that darkens counsel by words without knowledge?
Dress for action like a man;
I will question you, and you make it known to me.
Where were you when I laid the foundation of the earth?
Tell me, if you have understanding.
Who determined its measurements—surely you know!
Or who stretched the line upon it?
On what were its bases sunk,
or who laid its cornerstone,
when the morning stars sang together
and all the sons of God shouted for joy?
Or who shut in the sea with doors
when it burst out from the womb,
when I made clouds its garment
and thick darkness its swaddling band,
and prescribed limits for it
and set bars and doors,
and said, 'Thus far shall you come, and no farther,
and here shall your proud waves be stayed'?" (38:1–11)

1. *The Lord says Job has words without knowledge. Has Job spoken falsely about God? If so, why?*

2. *Why is it significant that the Lord questions Job instead of the other way around?*

3. What are the answers to the Lord's questions to Job?

DAY TWO READING AND QUESTIONS

And the LORD said to Job:
> "Shall a faultfinder contend with the Almighty?
>> He who argues with God, let him answer it."

Then Job answered the LORD and said:
> "Behold, I am of small account; what shall I answer you?
>> I lay my hand on my mouth.
> I have spoken once, and I will not answer;
>> twice, but I will proceed no further." (40:1–5)

1. Why does the Lord call Job a faultfinder? With whom does Job find fault?

2. How can Job answer God?

3. Why does Job think he is small?

DAY THREE READING AND QUESTIONS

Then Job answered the LORD and said:
> "I know that you can do all things,
>> and that no purpose of yours can be thwarted.
> 'Who is this that hides counsel without knowledge?'
> Therefore I have uttered what I did not understand,
>> things too wonderful for me, which I did not know.
> 'Hear, and I will speak;
>> I will question you, and you make it known to me.'
> I had heard of you by the hearing of the ear,
>> but now my eye sees you;

> therefore I despise myself,
>> and repent in dust and ashes." (42:1–6)

1. What does Job admit about his responses to his situation?

2. Why is it significant that Job sees God?

3. Job repents. Does this mean Job has sinned (as his friends said)? If not, what does it mean?

DAY FOUR READING AND QUESTIONS

After the Lord had spoken these words to Job, the Lord said to Eliphaz the Temanite: "My anger burns against you and against your two friends, for you have not spoken of me what is right, as my servant Job has. Now therefore take seven bulls and seven rams and go to my servant Job and offer up a burnt offering for yourselves. And my servant Job shall pray for you, for I will accept his prayer not to deal with you according to your folly. For you have not spoken of me what is right, as my servant Job has." So Eliphaz the Temanite and Bildad the Shuhite and Zophar the Naamathite went and did what the Lord had told them, and the Lord accepted Job's prayer.

And the Lord restored the fortunes of Job, when he had prayed for his friends. And the Lord gave Job twice as much as he had before. Then came to him all his brothers and sisters and all who had known him before, and ate bread with him in his house. And they showed him sympathy and comforted him for all the evil that the Lord had brought upon him. And each of them gave him a piece of money and a ring of gold.

And the Lord blessed the latter days of Job more than his beginning. And he had 14,000 sheep, 6,000 camels, 1,000 yoke of oxen, and 1,000 female donkeys. He had also seven sons and three daughters. And he called the name of the first daughter Jemimah, and the name of the second Keziah, and the name of the third Keren-happuch. And in all the land there were no women so beautiful as Job's daughters. And their father gave them an inheritance among their brothers. And after this Job lived 140 years, and saw his sons, and his sons' sons, four generations. And Job died, an old man, and full of days. (42:7–17)

1. Did Job speak what is right about the Lord?

2. Why does the Lord accept Job's prayers for the friends but not their own prayers?

3. How much does the Lord bless Job at the end?

DAY FIVE READING AND QUESTIONS

Go back and read Job 38:1–11; 40:1–5; 42:1–17.

1. Does Job get an answer from the Lord? What is that answer?

2. Does the Lord agree that Job is innocent?

3. Do the Lord's blessings on Job at the end make up for his suffering?

Meditation on Job 38:1–11; 40:1–5; 42:1–17

"I am God and you are not."

This is God's answer to Job. Job has suffered the loss of his children, his wealth, his health, and his friends, all because the Lord is trying to prove a point to Satan. The Lord even admits to Satan, "You incited me against him to destroy him without reason" (Job 2:3).

Are you satisfied with this "answer" from God? Don't you think Job deserves an explanation of what has happened to him? His wife has an explanation—Job is righteous, but God is not—so she urges Job to curse God and die. Job's friends have an answer—Job is not righteous, so the Lord has punished him.

But both answers are wrong, as Job knows. Job knows he is innocent, and he will not accuse the Lord of wrongdoing. How can this be? Job desperately wants an answer.

And he gets one. The Lord appears. The Lord does not explain, but he does show up. That is enough for Job.

"The patience of Job" is proverbial. Yet Job does not get the explanation he waits for. He gets the presence of God. And Job is willing to wait without any other answer.

Why do I believe in God? Because he has blessed me beyond my deserving. He is the God of love who has provided home and family and friends and food. But what if it all disappeared? Would I still believe in God?

Satan asks the question, "Does Job fear God for no reason?" The clear answer is yes. Even when it seems God has abandoned Job, Job does not abandon God. He trusts the God he does not understand.

Do we?

"God beyond all understanding, may we be content to see you, not understand you."

The Meditative Commentary Series
An exciting Bible study tool for your group

Matthew
by Gary Holloway
ISBN 978-0-97677-901-8

**1 & 2 Thessalonians,
1 & 2 Timothy, Titus**
by Gary Holloway
ISBN 978-0-89112-503-7

Acts of the Apostles
by Earl Lavender
ISBN 978-0-89112-501-3

Romans & Galatians
by Gary Holloway
ISBN 978-0-89112-502-0

Luke
by Earl Lavender
ISBN 978-0-89112-500-6

1 & 2 Corinthians
by Earl Lavender
ISBN 978-0-89112-568-6

**Ephesians, Philippians,
Colossians, & Philemon**
by Earl Lavender
ISBN 978-0-89112-561-7

LEAFWOOD
PUBLISHERS
an imprint of Abilene Christian University Press

Twelve Volumes Covering the New Testament

Hebrews & James
by Gary Holloway
ISBN 978-0-89112-505-1

John
by Gary Holloway
ISBN 978-0-89112-504-4

Mark
by Earl Lavender
ISBN 978-0-89112-551-8

The Letters of Peter, John, & Jude
by Gary Holloway
ISBN 978-0-89112-557-0

Revelation
by Terry Briley
ISBN 978-0-89112-559-4

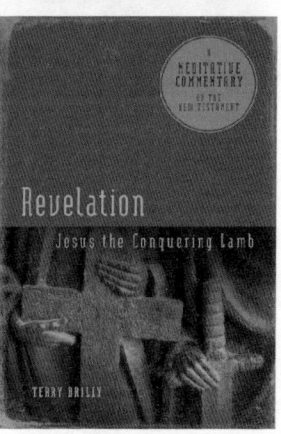

Do you want a deeper, more fulfilling way of Bible study? Do you want to know God through Scripture—not just to know the teachings but to have a relationship with the Teacher? This meditative commentary is for you. There are many commentaries on the books of the Bible, but this series is different. It employs the classic Christian method of "holy reading" to help you hear the voice of God.

Holy reading involves slowly engaging a short passage of Scripture, listening closely, reading repeatedly, praying the words, and perhaps sharing with fellow believers. God will bless us, our families, and our churches if we take the time to be still, listen, and do his word.

www.leafwoodpublishers.com

Also from Gary Holloway

LIVING GOD'S LOVE
An Invitation to Christian Spirituality

ISBN 9780974844121

A life richer than you can imagine

Do you want a deeper relationship with God? A closer walk with Jesus? A sense of the Holy Spirit's constant presence? Is this the deepest desire of your heart, but you don't know where to begin? This book is for you. It offers no shortcuts or sure-fire techniques for a deeper spirituality. But it serves as a simple and easy-to-follow signpost marking the path of daily relationship with God.

God invites you into relationship with him, just as you are. Even if you're not sure about God, even if you have no religious background, even if you've been a churchgoer all your life, God invites you to share his very life. It is a life richer than you can imagine.

"At last: a book that brings the essential subject of spiritual formation down to earth. Clear, reverent, practical, and warm."
—**Brian McLaren,** author of *A Generous Orthodoxy* and *Faith after Doubt*

"This profoundly simple book grounds the practices of spiritual maturing in a sound theology of relation in and with God. The result is not a simple formula for instant spirituality but healthy food for the soul."
—**Randy Harris,** author of *Living Jesus* and *Daring Faith*

1-877-816-4455 toll free
www.leafwoodpublishers.com

LEAFWOOD
PUBLISHERS
an imprint of Abilene Christian University Press

A MEDITATIVE COMMENTARY
on the Old Testament

PSALMS

Hymns of God's People

ISBN 978-1-68426-261-8

Express Your Feelings in Biblical Words

The Psalms are the hymnbook of Israel and the church, revealing how we experience the shape of grief, thankfulness, repentance, remembrance, and future hope. We need these words to survive in our world.

Psalms: Hymns of God's People is an invitation to hear God's voice in personal daily Bible study as well as in communal readings with fellow believers. Join Dr. Holloway and begin to grow in your ability to meditate on the Psalms. Learn to bring your requests to the heart of God and develop your relationship with Jesus. Allow the Spirit to give language to your cries for justice and concerns about the brokenness of our world.

"Gary Holloway is a master of simple prose that gets to the heart of things and draws readers in. Here he has applied that skill to produce a rich but simple tool to make the Psalms—the believer's prayerbook—a regular part of one's life with God."

—**Leonard Allen,** author of *Poured Out: The Spirit of God Empowering the Mission of God*

1-877-816-4455 toll free
www.leafwoodpublishers.com

LEAFWOOD
PUBLISHERS
an imprint of Abilene Christian University Press